# Entrepreneur

## QUICK GUIDE

# BECOMING
## A
# FRANCHISE
# OWNER

### TIM PARMETER

Entrepreneur Press, Publisher
Cover Design: Andrew Welyczko
Production and Composition: Alan Barnett Design

**Library of Congress Cataloging-in-Publication Data**
Names: Parmeter, Tim, author.
Title: Becoming a franchise owner / by Tim Parmeter.
Description: Santa Ana, CA : Entrepreneur Press, [2025] | Includes index. | Summary: "This step-by-step guide provides you with the tools and roadmap to becoming a successful franchise owner"— Provided by publisher.
Identifiers: LCCN 2024031186 (print) | LCCN 2024031187 (ebook) | ISBN 9781642011753 (paperback) | ISBN 9781613084854 (epub)
Subjects: LCSH: Franchises (Retail trade) | New business enterprises.
Classification: LCC HF5429.23 .P37 2025 (print) | LCC HF5429.23 (ebook) | DDC 658.8/708—dc23/eng/20240709
LC record available at https://lccn.loc.gov/2024031186
LC ebook record available at https://lccn.loc.gov/2024031187

# Table of Contents

# Introduction

Are you 100 percent in control over your personal and professional life? Are you in control of the way you spend your time?

What about this ...

Are you sick of working for someone else? Are you stuck in a career where you feel like you could be running the company more effectively? Are you tired of working long hours to help make someone else rich? Do you think you could make better decisions than those above you? And do you want to be the one making those decisions?

Not everybody does, and that is okay. But if you are nodding along to those questions, you have just picked up the right book.

On the flip side, maybe you are one of those rare people who actually likes their job. But perhaps you want to figure out how to build different revenue streams, diversify your portfolio, create a legacy opportunity for your family, or give yourself an exit strategy should the day ever come that you *don't* like your job anymore.

Or, although this may be hard to imagine, maybe you want to prepare yourself for the day when your current employer doesn't want *you* anymore. Then what?

> **"If your salary is your only source of income, you're one step away from poverty."**
>
> —*Warren Buffett*

Let's be honest here: You probably didn't stumble upon this book by accident. There was something about franchising that attracted your attention.

Maybe you have heard a little bit about franchising before but have been scared off by stories of high investment costs. Let me guess—you don't have $3 million under your mattress, do you?

But what if we told you that you didn't need that? What if we told you that franchising doesn't take millions of dollars? What if we told you that it can be more attainable than buying a starter home? What if we told you that you don't even have to own a franchise in an industry you know something about? What if we told you that you could become a franchise owner AND keep your current job?

If someone told you all of that, would you want to learn more? If so, that is what we are going to do in this book: dispel the myths and properly educate you on franchise ownership to determine whether this is the right path for you.

Frankly, what is the worst that could happen? Worst-case scenario, you read a book and learn something new. That is not going to kill you. But maybe, just maybe, you read this book and realize that franchise ownership is attainable for you. And perhaps you will even discover how to make that dream a reality.

Let me guess—when you hear the word "franchising," you probably think of the golden arches. McDonald's and its big-name fellows like Taco Bell and Burger King might be the quintessential examples of franchises, but they are far from representative of the franchising world as a whole. Unfortunately, many people don't realize just how diverse and accessible franchising really is.

It's no wonder why. After all, to become a McDonald's franchisee, you will need a minimum of $500,000 in liquid assets. Plus, the company reports that the initial investment cost can be as high as $2.3 million. To start a Taco Bell, you will need up to $2.9 million as an initial investment.

Hold on a second. Don't close this book yet.

Perhaps the most common myth about franchising is that it is all fast food and all uber-expensive. But as you are about to find out, that level of investment is the exception, not the rule—and fast food is only one of hundreds of different industries and niches that are franchised.

Guess what? You don't need $2 million in cash to start a franchise. In fact, there are thousands of companies out there that offer franchise-based business models with a *significantly* smaller price tag.

Franchises exist in many industries you may never have considered—there are over 4,000 franchisors in over 200 different industries in the U.S. alone. There are models in which franchise owners can be full-time or part-time. They can be active or very passive. They can be consumer-focused or business-focused—or both. They can work with skilled labor, unskilled labor, or no labor at all. And there are **Franchise Fees** and investment costs to fit all different budgets.

Up to this point, you have probably been working for someone else. Maybe the paycheck is alright, but you are tired of decisions that are not being carried out properly. You want the control, freedom, and flexibility to skip out early to go to your kid's soccer game, and you are done with being guilted for using your hard-earned vacation days to take a three-day weekend.

Franchise ownership will afford you all of that and more. So why doesn't everyone become a franchise owner? Great question.

Brands are constantly looking for new owners who are dedicated, motivated, and excited to succeed. If you are reading this book, you have already taken a step in the right direction, and you just might be the perfect candidate that a franchise is looking for.

Now that you know you don't need to be a multimillionaire to own a franchise, you are probably wondering what other qualifications are required. You might be wondering if you have the right industry knowledge, the right degree, or the right management experience.

Here is another trade secret: You don't need any of that.

That's right: None of those qualifications are requirements. We have worked with plenty of clients turned franchise owners who do not hold a four-year degree, have not worked in management, and are not already experts in the world of lawn care, cutting hair, senior services, picking up dog poo (yes, there are actual franchises for that), or whatever other industry they are about to enter.

This might sound crazy, but it is the truth. In corporate America, there is so much emphasis placed on your career trajectory and your industry experience rather than on your actual talents, skills, and the core values that make you who you are. But when you step out of that bubble, you will realize that franchising offers opportunities for everyone out there—that is, everyone who is motivated to take charge of their careers and their lives, ready to learn, and excited to execute a franchisor's plan.

On Sunday night, are you already dreading Monday morning? Do you often wake up in the morning and feel the stress of your job hit you before you even leave your house? Maybe your job is just fine, pays the bills, and is worth eight or nine hours of your time every weekday. But maybe, just maybe, you long for something more from your career and your life.

Maybe you would like a little more control, whether that is over your hours, your lifestyle, your involvement, the money you make, or your leadership opportunities. Maybe you would like the chance to contribute to your community and become the face of your own business. Maybe you have always dreamed of starting something that is all your own.

If this sounds like you, it is time to find a path that makes you *excited* to get out of bed in the morning, *excited* to go to work, and *excited* to build something for yourself and your family. In short, it is time to find a path that allows you control over your life. There is no better time to take the first step toward creating your better tomorrow. There is no better time to consider franchise ownership.

In the course of this book, we will answer all of your burning questions about franchise ownership, including:

- What is franchising?
- Why do people become franchise owners?
- Who can become a franchise owner?
- What prior experience do I need?
- Which industries are the best for franchising?
- How do I choose the right franchise?
- Can I afford franchise ownership?
- How much money will I make?
- What does this process look like?
- And so much more.

If any of these questions pique your interest, you are in the right place. And we are excited to help you get started on your journey.

### *So Who Am I?*

If you have gotten this far, you are probably wondering where all of this advice on franchise ownership is coming from. Let me introduce myself.

My name is Tim Parmeter, and I am the founder and CEO of FranCoach, a national search firm dedicated to working with individuals who are interested in owning a franchise. Our company is partnered with over 600 of the top franchisors in the country, spanning nearly 70 industries, and we have worked with hundreds of individuals to help each of them find the perfect franchise to own.

Our #1 goal is to properly educate people on franchise ownership to help them determine IF franchise ownership is for them. If so, then we work to find the absolute best franchise for them to own.

So why me? Why should you trust the advice and information that I am going to share throughout these pages?

I have been where you are. I understand the fear you are probably feeling. But here is my perspective: There is nothing to be lost from education. I want to guide you in your journey through this book as you explore whether or not franchise ownership is the right path for you.

Maybe you shouldn't do this. But before you make that decision, you deserve to be properly informed on what franchise ownership is really all about—because maybe, just maybe, this IS the right path for you.

By the time you are done reading, you will be equipped with new information and knowledge that will allow you to make confident decisions regarding franchise ownership. You will develop a strong understanding of the who, what, where, why, and how of this topic, and I will be by your side every step of the way.

Are you ready to take the first steps toward creating your better tomorrow? If so, just turn the page.

Or don't. If you don't want to turn the page, then don't do it. But you bought this book ... so you are probably committed to more than just a page or two.

---

## CHAPTER 1

# Why Should I Become a Franchise Owner?

### What Is Franchising?

Let's go back to the beginning and make sure that we are on the same page when it comes to the concept at the core of this book: franchising. In simple terms, what exactly is it?

People sometimes describe franchising as a "business in a box." It is a proven and systematic method of working for yourself. The training, systems, and plans are all in place just waiting for you to arrive and follow along.

Instead of being the creator of everything (as you would be if you started a business from scratch), you are the implementer of a tried-and-true strategy and the owner of an established brand. And, as we will discuss in a few pages, there are plenty of benefits.

Franchising also involves a relationship between a **franchisor** and a **franchisee**. Let's break it down so that we all understand the role of each of these parties.

The **franchisor** is the brand. They create the business from scratch and hope it works. Then, they establish the brand's trademark or trade name, and put together a business system that will typically include brand standards, values, systems, and support.

They also provide resources and guidance for franchise owners in their systems in order to set them up for success.

A good franchisor does not spring up overnight. There are years of building the initial business, scaling, and plenty of trial and error needed just to start the process of becoming a franchise. And once that is completed, it takes hundreds of thousands of dollars and years of planning to be ready to take on franchise owners. In other words, the franchisor has done TONS of legwork in order to set its franchise owners up for success—and, as an owner, you get to benefit from those efforts.

The **franchisee** is the individual on the other side of the equation. That person will pay an initial fee and then ongoing royalties to the franchisor. A new franchise owner is paying for the right to do business using the franchisor's name and their proven system, which encompasses numerous processes and plenty of industry knowledge in areas such as training, support, marketing expertise, software, vendor relations, and more.

When explaining this concept to clients, we often describe the arrangement between the franchisor and the franchisee as similar to a parent-child relationship. The franchisor gives the franchisee (that is you) the game plan. They tell you how to properly execute everything, and they promise to be there and support you along the way. They tell you how to do your marketing and help you with many different aspects of running the business.

As the franchisee, your number one duty is to follow the plan. The franchisor is the creator and tester of all things, and you are tasked with implementing and executing a proven, successful game plan.

## DEFINITION

**Franchising** is a mutually beneficial agreement between a franchisee and a franchisor. The franchisor allows the franchisee to use its trade name and operating methods in exchange for a portion of the sales. The franchisee operates the business according to the terms of the contract. This arrangement is reminiscent of a parent-child relationship in that the franchisor provides a proven plan and the franchisee is responsible for following it.

### What Is the #1 Reason People Become Franchise Owners?

Now you have a clearer picture of what franchising means. So why do people become franchise owners?

The answer is probably not what you think. It's not money, although franchising can certainly be lucrative and financially rewarding.

The short answer? Control.

### Control Over What?

Don't worry, the fact that you want to get into the franchising business does not make you a control freak. But the number one reason that people become franchise owners is control—and that means control over many different aspects of life. Franchising is a pathway that affords you control over ...

## Your Schedule

As a parent, the flexibility of franchise ownership is something I appreciate in my own life—but, whether or not you have children, flexibility is one of the greatest gifts of franchising. As a business owner, your time is within your control. You can head to the gym in the middle of the day. You can work unconventional hours. You can schedule meetings only while your kids are in school—and you can make sure you're free to take them to their activities. Instead of canceling plans with friends to cater to your boss's needs, you can put **your** needs (and wants) first.

## Your Lifestyle

I was talking with a guy the other day who hates his job and knows he wants to franchise—but his wife was not necessarily on board. She was worried about him walking away from his salary, but it was also about their lifestyle. They have three kids and she wanted to know if he would still be able to coach their sports teams.

"Are you kidding me?" I said. "You're absolutely going to be able to do that." How? Well, if you have your son's baseball practice or game on Thursday at 6 o'clock, you are not going to schedule a meeting on Thursday at 6 o'clock. When you are a franchise owner, you have control over how you spend your time.

## Time With Your Family

For so many people we talk to, one of the biggest frustrations of the corporate world is the constraints it places on time with their families. Have you ever missed a ballet recital, a soccer game, or a school event for work? Have you ever had to work late on a Friday or clock extra hours over the weekend because your boss needs that big project completed? As a franchise owner, you will have control—and you can use that control to prioritize the people who mean the most to you.

### Your Income

Believe it or not, money is rarely the first thing people say when asked why they want to become a franchise owner. But you will have control over how much or how little you earn. If you want to make more, you are in control of that. As an employee, you don't get much of a say in your compensation. But as an owner, you can keep growing and expanding by adding multiple units or even multiple brands. If you want to grow an empire, that is a real possibility.

On the flip side, if you get to a point where you are comfortable with the money you make and want to stay right there, you can do that as a franchise owner, too. A franchisor is never going to push you or demand that you make 20 percent more next year (like an employer might). At the end of the day, franchisors want their franchisees to be happy.

### Your Freedom

Want to take a vacation? Want to spend more time with your family? Want to get more involved in your community? As a franchise owner, you have the ultimate freedom when it comes to these things—and so many more. Finally, you will not have to ask someone else's permission to do what you want with your own life.

### The People You Are Around

Control does not start and end with your lifestyle. You get the chance to decide whom you work with. You get control over whom you surround yourself with, too. This encompasses all the people involved in your business: your staff, your customers, your community, and even the franchisor and their team. You are in the driver's seat when it comes to surrounding yourself with people you trust and want to partner with to build your business.

### Your Role as an Owner

Franchise ownership is not a one-size-fits-all situation. There are many different roles that franchise owners take on. Some franchises offer **semi-absentee models** whereby you can even keep your current job and take on franchise work part-time. The options are much more diverse than what you would see in a traditional corporate job.

As an owner, you are in control over what you do every day. In fact, there is nothing more important than the owner's role, because you determine the best franchise for YOU to own. What are you truly good at? What do you enjoy doing? What transferable skills have you already acquired that you can take with you? What would you prefer not to do, or to do less of? You are the boss—so take this opportunity to make your skill set shine and design a career that is perfectly suited to your strengths, goals, and priorities.

### Your Community

You get to choose whom you hire and whom you work with. But you also get to choose the location of your franchise and how you interact with the community there. You might even get a chance to establish yourself as a recognizable face in your local area.

Part of selecting your community is getting the chance to determine the core values of your business. You will be able to get involved with your community and take part in activities, groups, or causes that are important to you. For instance, you might sponsor a Little League team or start a cycling group—as a business owner, your efforts can go so much further than they would as an individual working on your own.

Think of those "Toys for Tots" boxes you see pop up around the holidays—do you ever see those boxes on someone's front porch? No, you see that at someone's business. The boxes are there because that cause is important to the owner.

### Your Priorities

You have the ability to decide what comes first in your life and then shape your day-to-day activities to adhere to those priorities. That is not something that many people in corporate jobs can claim for themselves. But as a franchise owner, you have control over your own life.

### Your Growth

In the corporate world, you are eventually going to hit a ceiling—if you have not already. But with franchising, there will always be the opportunity for growth. If you want to make more, you can work harder, you can expand, you can get additional units or additional franchise brands. Basically, you can build a franchise empire as large (or as small) as you want.

As they say in *Finding Nemo,* "Just keep swimming, just keep swimming." But in this case, just keep growing, just keep growing, just keep growing …

## And So Much More

All of these areas of control are becoming more and more important to us in the modern world. Plus, for those of us who have to go into the office, there are the issues of traffic, lengthy commutes, and missing out on time with our friends and families. Whatever area you are looking to regain control over, franchising may be an attractive option.

Most of the clients who come to us at FranCoach looking for help getting started in the franchising world are wanting the same thing: a life that offers them more control. Franchising can be an incredibly rewarding pathway to becoming a business owner and to living the life you want.

## What Does Control Really Mean?

So, what are some of the things we hear when we're talking to people about control? Many people who come to us have a story that goes something like this:

"I'm working my butt off for somebody else, making decent money, but not making as much as the person in charge of the whole company. So, if I'm going to work my tail off, then I want to be able to reap the rewards."

Some of that is about the flexibility and freedom to really control your time. But it is also about being able to decide how you might grow things within your business in the future.

Some of the happiest franchise owners in any franchise are not necessarily the top performers. Now, that may seem kind of counterintuitive. If they are not the top performers, why are they the happiest people?

Of course, the answer is **control**. They are working the amount of time they want to work, and they are making an amount of money that they are comfortable with. Once you reach your status quo like that as a franchise owner, you are good. You are set. And that is really not something you can do in the corporate world. The franchisor is not going to hound you (like your boss does) to get 20 percent more revenue next year. Franchisors want happy franchisees—so, if you are happy, they are happy.

On the flip side, what is your growth potential? In the corporate world, you can work as hard as you want, but there are so many other factors in play and there is only so high up the ladder that you are going to climb. As a franchise owner, you are in control of the growth.

Your work and dedication to the business are going to make that initial single unit grow and become prosperous and profitable for you. But where can you go from there? You can have multiple units. Does that mean multiple locations of a retail franchise? Possibly. Does it mean multiple territories of a non-retail franchise? Absolutely.

You may be able to add additional products and services to a brand. You could go from owning a single unit to two units or three—or even a whole city, state, or region. All of those things are possible and you are in control of them, not somebody else.

Want to go crazy? What about owning franchises in multiple brands? You can continue to grow. Think about it like this: In the corporate world, you cannot have two full-time jobs. Imagine deciding to be the VP of Sales at two different companies (although, if you can figure out how to pull that off, let us know).

But, in all seriousness, you *can* be the owner of two separate businesses. And you can grow them accordingly, in the way you want, because **you are in control**.

## Is Franchise Ownership Attainable?

"This all sounds pretty good," you're probably thinking, "but is franchise ownership actually a possibility for me?"

There are countless myths and misconceptions about franchising that hold many people back from ever exploring this avenue, many of which we will dispel in this book. In reality, franchising is more attainable than you probably realize.

We touched on the financial aspect briefly (and don't worry, we will dive deeper into that topic a bit later) but, in short, franchising **does not** require millions of dollars in net worth or a massive pile of cash to get started. There are numerous pathways to making the dream of franchise ownership a reality from the financial side of the equation. More often than not, it costs a lot less than you might think.

Franchising is also **not** all fast food. Yes, McDonald's, Taco Bell, and Wendy's are classic examples that people might name when asked to list franchises, but the franchising world is much broader than many people realize. There are brands in industries like health and wellness, fitness, business services, home repair, advertising, employment, tech, senior care, and more. If you are thinking that you do not want to be standing over a fryer all day … good. That is not what franchise ownership looks like (even for a restaurant owner).

And finally, franchise ownership does not require a degree in business or years' worth of management training. Age, education levels, previous resumé fillers ... none of those matters. Franchisors have created the playbook for you. All you have to do is come in and execute a proven plan. You will have extensive support on your side as you embark on your journey to become a business owner.

If you are worried that you are not qualified to own a franchise, don't be. There are options out there for pretty much everyone, regardless of budget, background, and any other considerations.

In the next section, we will dive deeper into the pressing question that is on many aspiring business owners' minds: **Who can become a franchise owner?**

## CHAPTER 2

# Do I Need Industry Experience?

### Do You Need Any Specific Industry Background, Education, or Skills to Become a Franchise Owner?

Nope.

### How Is That Possible?

Many people who aspire to be business owners get hung up on myths about why they *can't* accomplish this goal.

Really, the word *can't* is just masking fear of the unknown, and this fear is what holds us back. Oftentimes, greatness is just on the other side of this fear—and all we need to conquer it is more information. With that in mind, here is the truth:

Franchise ownership is very accessible—all we need to conquer it is more information. With that in mind, let's break down a few of the myths that might be holding you back from truly imagining your success as a franchise owner.

### Myth #1: Franchise owners need industry experience.

Cue an annoying buzzer sound here—WRONG! Franchise owners do *not* need experience in the industry their franchise is situated in. It is easy to understand why many people think this. In the corporate world, industry experience and a lengthy resumé or LinkedIn profile are everything. But, when it comes to franchising, the opposite is true.

Think about it like this: A franchise owner is rarely the *doer*. You are not going to be the person who is flipping the burgers or making the donuts. Are there some franchises out there that are really designed that way? Absolutely. But those are for people who are looking for that. The vast majority of franchise owners are not the *doers* in their brands.

And that is the way that franchisors like it. Consider the home services industry, for instance. The franchise will have a crew on the truck, and the franchisor does not want you on the truck. Or, if you have a restaurant, you are not going to be the one in the kitchen making everything. If you are, who is going to be running the business?

In fact, most people end up owning a franchise in an industry they have little or no experience in. We have had accountants start lawn care franchises, pilots start construction franchises, and an individual who is the self-described "biggest slob on the planet" start a cleaning franchise. And the list goes on! You don't need to have senior care experience, for example, to own a franchise in that booming industry.

Franchisors are typically not looking for owners with specific industry experience. They are seeking talented individuals to work ON the business rather than IN the business. Franchisors also offer very extensive training and support programs to educate the owners on their new industry.

### *Myth #2: Franchise owners need executive career experience.*

There are certainly plenty of franchise owners who are seasoned executives coming from the corporate world. But do you need to have spent the last 15 years as a vice president to be a franchise owner? Absolutely not.

I don't know that I have ever heard a franchisor ask to see someone's resumé. And that can be freeing for people who are coming from a corporate culture where your resumé is everything. When your resumé is the be-all and end-all of your career, it is easy to get stuck in one lane, right? Let's say that you are the VP of Sales at a manufacturing company and then you try to get a VP of Sales job at a company in another industry. They are probably going to say that you do not have any experience—or that you do not have the *right* experience. But come on … it's sales and sales management. How could none of your skills be transferable?

There is a certain element of brainwashing in the corporate world when it comes to your resumé and career experience. But in franchising, it is often liberating for people to find out that we are going to build out their perfect role from scratch.

It might be cheesy, but we always ask clients, "What is your dream scenario? What do you want to be when you grow up?" Now, we would pose these same questions to you. Why? If you are living your best life and enjoying the professional career of your dreams, you are probably not two chapters deep into a guide about franchise ownership.

So, if they are not looking for job experience, what are franchisors looking for? If you ask any franchise what they are looking for in an owner, they will all say the same exact two things:

1. Someone who will follow a proven plan
2. Someone who will put forth the required effort

Now, "required effort" could be semi-absentee ownership and mean just 10 to 15 hours per week, but you still *have* to do it. Each brand will give you some additional specifics for their particular franchise, but those two criteria reign supreme.

### Myth #3: Franchise owners need millions of dollars.

Not so much. Let's be honest: Not many people have millions of dollars just lying around. A large number of the clients we have worked with at FranCoach have an overall net worth far less than $1 million. In fact, the average single unit **Total Investment** (more on "Total Investment" later) of the franchises we work with is around $200,000—and there are several franchises with a Total Investment of under $100,000.

Think of owning a franchise like buying a house: The actual cash needed to start a franchise is only a portion of the Total Investment, just like your down payment is only a portion of what you need to buy your house. There are many different funding options available, which we will discuss in Chapter 5. Funding is just one way to open up more potential paths for you to start your new business.

So how much money is enough? The analogy we like to use is "Can you buy a cute little starter home in Topeka, Kansas?" In other words, do you have $20,000 or $30,000 for that down payment? Would you be able to get a home loan and still have a little bit of money left over to buy curtains and pay the movers? If so, there are hundreds of franchises that fit that financial profile. There will be funding options for you if that is your situation.

Will $20,000 get you six Taco Bells? No, it will not. But will it get you in the game and offer you literally hundreds of opportunities? Yes.

In summary, there are very few restrictions on who can become a franchise owner. If you set your mind to the task and are motivated to succeed, you are likely an eligible candidate.

## Should I Own a Franchise in My Passion Area?

We have established that you do not need industry experience to own a franchise, but what about passion? Do you need to have a passion for what a franchise does to be the owner of that franchise?

The short answer is … no. That does not mean you can't have a passion, but passion is a huge myth in franchising.

Let's say you are "passionate" about fitness. We often have clients who say, "I am passionate about fitness. Therefore, I need to own a fitness franchise." Is that possible? It is absolutely possible. Is it required? Absolutely not.

One of the key pieces of this puzzle is that, as a franchise owner, again, you are typically not the *doer*. For instance, if you own a pet-related franchise, you are not going to be the person walking the dogs. You are in charge of this franchise, remember? You are going to be focused on running that business and making it successful.

That "it" factor of your passion is not really what is going to make you successful. The real question you should ask is what are you doing day in and day out as a business owner? That is the key.

We are not saying that your passion for an industry does not matter. Sometimes, the person with a huge passion for (and background in) fitness ends up owning a fitness franchise. But this scenario happens much less often than you might think.

You want to think about the things that you will be doing as an owner and how you will be spending your time in the business—your tasks, so to speak. You want to ask yourself numerous questions about what your day-to-day life owning the business will look like.

Now you know that you do not need industry experience. You do not even need to have a passion for the industry that your franchise is in. That might seem overwhelming—suddenly, there are thousands of potential options. So how will you know which one is right?

Pinpointing your ideal day-to-day life as an owner is a crucial piece of determining not the best franchise in general but the best franchise for YOU to own. In the next section, we will dive deeper into figuring out your unique, individualized pathway to success.

CHAPTER 3

# Choosing the Right Franchise

## How Do People *Think* Choosing a Franchise Works?

When it comes to choosing the right franchise, there are countless misconceptions about how the process works. Why? Because the **Discovery Process** of finding the right franchise is totally different from the typical, corporate job search process.

You already know how to hunt for a job, right? You think about what you have done in the past. You list out all of your roles and titles in that document we call a resumé. And then, based on your past experience, you figure out what jobs you can realistically apply for.

Maybe you are looking at industries—in the corporate world, the industry you have previously worked in is pretty much the only one you even have a remotely realistic chance of successfully interviewing in. That idea leads us into the four common misconceptions that we see all too often from our clients at FranCoach.

First, so many people come to us saying something like this: "I have to own a franchise in an industry that I have experience in."

Wrong.

We will dive into this more throughout this section of the book, but your prior industry experience has pretty much nothing to do with the franchise that's right for you.

Second on the list, let's talk about Google. You might have done some Google searches that look something like this:
"What is the best franchise for me to own?"
- "What are the hottest franchises this year?"
- "List of the best franchises"

Let me give you a little tip right now ... stop Googling! Google is not your friend and lists of the "best" or "hottest" franchises are **ALMOST ALWAYS** a myth. Don't fall for it.

Third, we have a little bit of confirmation bias going on. When you think of a "franchise," you think of the things you know and see. You drive past a McDonald's on the way to work, so that is what "franchise" means to you. There are so many options out there (remember, there are over 4,000 franchise brands in the U.S. alone) so don't box yourself into what's right in front of you. As you embark on the franchise Discovery Process, you want to keep an open mind and realize that franchising is a much broader world than you have probably ever imagined.

And finally, one of the biggest misconceptions about franchise ownership is that you have to own a franchise in an industry you are "passionate" about. We touched on this misconception in Chapter 2—loving dogs does not mean you have to own a pet franchise. Being a gym junkie does not mean you need to own a fitness franchise.

Clients bring up all these misconceptions—and then some!—all the time when we start the Discovery Process at FranCoach, during which we match clients with some brands they may be compatible with. More often than not, the franchise they end up owning is:

- in an industry they have little to no experience in;
- something that was not even on their radar when they began the search; and
- oftentimes, a franchise they did not even know existed.

We will dive deeper into all of these myths in this section of the book, but now that you know how choosing the right franchise does NOT work, let's discuss the real version of this process.

### How Does Choosing a Franchise ACTUALLY Work?

We have said it before, and we will say it again: Finding the best franchise for you is NOTHING like searching for a traditional, corporate job.

Instead of considering your previous experience and then following those threads to a job that aligns with what you have already been doing, you get to **reverse engineer** your ideal career. And the best part of this? You get to …

### Be Selfish.

Ever since we were little kids, we were told NOT to be selfish. But get this … when it comes to finding YOUR best franchise to own, your mom was wrong. It is 100 percent okay to be selfish.

In fact, it is not just okay—it is actually required. How fun is that?

Why does finding the right franchise require being a little (or a lot) selfish? In the corporate world, your next job is based on what you have previously done and in what industry. Your career is all-too-often based on what you can get rather than what you really want.

Franchise ownership, on the other hand, is all about creating your dream scenario. It sounds a little cheesy, but it is true. If you were not longing for something more or something different, let's be honest—you probably would not be considering franchise ownership.

Instead of focusing on your past (your prior jobs, your corporate industry), you get to focus on your **future**. You get to build the career you want, all while taking control of your life, your finances, your schedule, and so much more.

When it comes to finding the right franchise for you, it all boils down to what we call the **"Get Out of Bed Test."**

### What Is the Get Out of Bed Test?

When we are working with clients, we talk a lot about the "Get Out of Bed Test." It might sound like corporate jargon, the kind of thing that people roll their eyes at—like "synergy" or "circle back." But I have found that, as time goes on, the meaning of this phrase becomes clearer to our clients.

As you look for the right franchise for YOU to own, you want to find an opportunity that will make you excited to get out of bed in the morning and to head out to work on your ideal business.

That all starts with the **owner role**. What are you going to do every day as an owner? Again, you get to be selfish here—but you also need to be honest with yourself.

Imagine that you are applying for a corporate role that requires 75 percent of your time to be devoted to business development. You may not have tons of skills in that area, but you need a job and the company seems decent, so you answer your interview questions as if you are the world's best business development person. Congrats! You tricked your interviewer into believing you and you got the job. Now, you get to take their money until you can find a better job … but ultimately, you are setting yourself up to be pretty miserable, because business development is something you are neither very good at nor particularly enjoy.

Now, let's compare that scenario to the process of finding the right franchise. Instead of tailoring your interview answers to someone else's job requirements, you get to build out your role as an owner and decide what is really important to you.

You might look at a franchise that wants an owner who will spend 75 percent of their time on business development. Maybe you looked at it because you worked in the industry, or you have a friend whose uncle's second cousin's sister owns that brand and is killing it, or you Googled "best franchises" and that one was on the list.

During the Discovery Process, you convince the franchise that you are great at business development and you love it—but again, you are lying to them and to yourself. This time, the consequences are far greater. You don't just have a job for the interim, you now OWN a business that requires a skill that you do not have or tasks you do not enjoy doing.

The business you own needs to be something that gets you out of bed in the morning. If you are doing something you do not like and that you are not that good at doing, how can you be successful as an owner? And more importantly, how happy will you be?

Exactly.

When you own a franchise, you are not just taking a job to avoid unemployment. This is YOUR business paid for with YOUR money. And that is where being selfish comes into play.

As you search for the ideal franchise for YOU to own, you have to look at this process through an entirely different lens.

Instead of considering what someone else wants from you,

consider what you want to do on a daily basis. This is truly a chance to have a blank slate.

What are you really good at? What do you really want to do every day? Nothing matters more than these two questions. Why? Because YOU are the one who has to get up and run YOUR franchise every day.

Think of it like this … would you hire yourself for the owner role the franchise is looking for? If not, it does not matter how successful all of that brand's other owners are. You won't be successful in that role. And, more importantly, you won't be happy.

As you think about your role as a franchise owner and the right franchise that fits with that role, there are a few key questions that you can ask yourself to discover what you really want.

## What Questions Should I Ask Myself?

In this section, we are going to pose some questions that you will want to ask yourself before you begin looking at different franchises. But remember this: It is okay if you do not know all of the answers to these questions right now. In fact, going through the franchise Discovery Process will help you consider your answers more fully.

To start, let's talk more about what you hope to get out of franchise ownership. What are your goals and priorities in this process? While you do not need to have everything entirely fleshed out, it is important to think about what you envision yourself doing every day.

Here are some questions worth thinking about as you begin looking into franchising. These questions will help you build out the criteria for your role as an owner as well as the perfect franchise for you to own:

- **What do you actually enjoy doing?** What are you good at? Note that we are not asking, "What have you done before?" The question is, "What do you want to do every single day?"
- **Who do you want to be around all day long?** In your past jobs, have there been certain people or certain roles that you worked better with, or enjoyed working with more? Or less? Have you ever wondered why a certain person was hired? Or not fired? Guess what … as a franchise owner, YOU are in charge of this. The people around you and the roles those people fill matter, and you get to choose what that looks like.
- **What type of customers do you want to have?** Wait, why does this matter? Again, this is YOUR business. Do you want a business that deals in high-volume, low-price products with a limited relationship with customers. Do you want a high-quality, big-ticket, project-based business? Do you want a membership business where you build strong relationships with recurring customers?

There is no wrong answer to any of these questions, but again, the main thing is that you have to be honest about what you want. If you are not sure, that is okay too. It is common to have openness in any of these areas as you start the process. Either way, figuring out the answers to these questions will ultimately help you find the best franchise to own.

**What about the franchisors themselves?** The whole point of a franchise is that the franchisor has a proven plan and system in place. They offer support in every area of a business and often in areas where people do not even realize there would be support. That said, not every franchise is the same in the type and levels of support that they offer. So, it's important to figure out where you need the most support. If you cannot spell SEO (let alone define what it means or know how to excel at it), you will need support there. If you are awesome at business development and hunting down customers, then that might not be as important. How will you know which franchise is good at what? Stay tuned, we'll get there.

**What about the people in the franchise?** We mentioned how important your staff and customers are, and surrounding yourself with the right people is key to your success and happiness as a franchise owner. This principle extends to the team on the franchisor side, too. How you connect with the franchise, their leadership and support teams, other franchise owners, their culture, and their values ... all of these factors matter greatly. In fact, for most people, interpersonal relationships are the second-most impactful aspect of the search beyond crafting the owner role.

We have had some clients at FranCoach over the years who are what you might call "Type A"—they will create detailed spreadsheets with numerous categories to compare and contrast different franchise brands. But what are the categories that everyone seems to forget on those comparison spreadsheets? Many people fail to think about (1) owner role and (2) franchisor culture and support. These are important considerations, and it is crucial not to overlook them.

### Why Doesn't My Industry Experience Matter?

As we talk about building out your ideal owner role as a franchise owner, you are probably wondering ... "Why doesn't my industry experience matter?"

The answer is simple: As a franchise owner, you are rarely the doer.

McDonald's owners do not make fries all day long. Therefore, they do not need resumés filled with fry-making experience. Or take one of my other favorite examples: You could be the biggest slob on the planet and own a cleaning franchise. Mind-blowing, right?

Get this: Over 90 percent of our clients at FranCoach end up owning a franchise that is in an industry they have little to no experience in.

Think about what would happen if you detoxed yourself from the short-sightedness of the corporate world. Think back to all of those jobs you thought about applying to, thought you might even be great at ... but did not have the right industry "experience" to even apply for. With that in mind, it is easy to see how refreshing the franchise world is.

Franchisors really do not care about what industry you have been in previously. They care about YOU: What you are good at, what you want to do all day, what you are all about as a human.

But wait ... how is that possible?

As the franchise owner, you are rarely the one actually doing the work all day. Let's go back to the cleaning example. The owner of a residential cleaning franchise is not cleaning houses all day. Even if you never, ever clean your own house yourself, it is not rocket science.

Plus, the franchisor will have a thorough training program detailing the proven methods they offer to give clients beautifully clean homes. Will you learn this method? Absolutely. Will you be the one dragging the mop around all day? Absolutely not.

"Okay," you're thinking, "but cleaning is a pretty simple thing to learn and understand. What if the franchise is in an industry that is a bit more challenging?"

I'll use the example of Great Clips, an affordable hair salon franchise. Sounds like a great opportunity, right? After all, this business is probably never going out of *style* (get it?). But what if you do not know how to cut hair? How can you own this type of business?

This should not be a shocker at this point ... but Great Clips is not looking for you, the owner, to cut hair. You are the owner, NOT the doer. Will you learn the basics of cutting hair? Absolutely. Are there hair-cutting considerations specific to that franchise? For sure, and you will learn them all. But you will not be the one cutting hair.

You can apply this same example to virtually any franchise. Think of electricians, plumbers, and the like. You'll learn some basics as the owner of a franchise in one of these sectors, but you are not going to be the one rewiring houses, unclogging drains, and the like.

So, if you are not doing the groundwork, what *is* your role? In short, whatever you want it to be. If you are the owner of a cleaning franchise, you might be out connecting in the community, building relationships with referral partners, and creating awareness for the business. You might be doing consultations with potential customers. You might be working on customer retention to ensure that you have happy customers who keep on coming back.

You will also be managing your staff. Using the cleaning example, you will be managing a largely unskilled staff and training them to clean according to the system of your given franchise brand. You will need to be good at and enjoy working with people, building relationships in the community, and training and managing an unskilled staff. But guess what you do NOT need to be good at? That's right: cleaning houses. Sure, you *could* do it ... but it is not your job.

The same logic applies to the plumbing example. This is a less personable, need-based business with a staff that is already highly skilled. As an owner, you might be connecting in the community to build referral partners like realtors, contractors, first responders, and other home services brands. You will also be managing a team of highly skilled, already trained master plumbers who are doing a job that you CANNOT and SHOULD NOT do.

The right franchise for you boils down to your preferences and skills. What type of staff do you prefer to manage? Skilled or unskilled? Or would you rather work with salespeople? What would you like to do every day as an owner? As always, this goes back to the **Get Out of Bed Test** that we mentioned earlier.

Make sure you are asking yourself the questions that really matter instead of falling down the Google rabbit hole.

### Why Isn't Google Our Friend?

Want to find a job? Want to find the best Mexican restaurant for dinner? Want to research a car to buy? Want to find a date for Friday night? You can use Google for all of these things. But what if you want to find the best franchise to own? Not so much.

Why is Google not the best source for this information? There are a few reasons.

First of all, a lot of what you are going to find online about a franchise centers around what it is like to be a customer. That's not exactly helpful when you are trying to find YOUR best franchise to own.

Second, as we have already learned, finding the best franchise to own is an incredibly individualized and personalized process. What is best for you might be terrible for me ... and vice versa.

Third, the most important factor in finding the best franchise to own is defining your role as an owner. Using the questions you explored earlier in this section and figuring out what role will make you excited to get out of bed every morning, you will be able to reverse engineer your dream career scenario. Unfortunately, this information is rarely something you will find online.

Plus, there are many behind-the-scenes aspects of each franchise: how they support you, their team, their culture, their vision, and more. You can Google all you want, but you are not going to find the answers on a public-facing web page.

Finally, there are unique franchising structures and setups that you will not find anything about online. For instance, many franchises offer a model known as "semi-absentee ownership," which allows you to keep your current job and own a franchise. (We'll talk more about this in Chapter 8.)

Google is even less helpful about semi-absentee ownership than it is about the plethora of other topics we have discussed. Why? First off, "semi-absentee" is one of the most poorly defined terms in franchising. If you asked 10 franchisors to define the term, you are likely to get about 13 different answers.

Ultimately, searching Google to try to find the perfect franchise for you to own often adds confusion, rather than clarity, into your journey.

If Google is not the best research option, however, you are probably wondering where to turn to get the information and education you need. This is where a franchise coach can come in to help. At the end of this section, we will address the topic of franchise coaches and how they can assist you in the process of finding the right franchise for you.

## What Am I Missing?

We talk to plenty of clients who come in with a preconceived idea of the type of business that they want to own. They will say something like:

- "When I was a kid, I wanted to own an X business."
- "I see X business all over, and it seems very successful."
- "I really like being a customer of X business, and therefore, I want to own one."

Are any of these statements things to ignore? Absolutely not. But does that mean your ideal franchise to own is one you are already had in mind? Again, absolutely not.

Finding the best franchise to own is a lot like dating. Say there's a girl in your neighborhood named Sarah. She is your age and you hang out in school. Therefore, you should get married. Is that possible? Sure. But basically, you are saying that Sarah is THE ONE because your search parameters for a wife extended to all of one subdivision.

Here is the question I suggest you think about: Do you want the best of what you know, or do you want what is absolutely best for you?

As you search for the right franchise for YOU to own, it is crucial to keep an open mind. More often than not, the ideal franchise for you is one that you might not have heard of or even thought of before.

## Can I Get Some Help?

With Google off the table and questions raised about pursuing a franchise in your passion area, you might be wondering where you *should* go to get reputable information about franchise ownership. Well, this book is a great place to start. But beyond that, there are a number of options that you might want to consider. A popular one is working with a franchise coach.

Most people have no idea that there is an entire industry designed to help people find the best franchise. Our team at FranCoach does this, and there are many other providers as well.

A franchise coach is someone who is extremely knowledgeable about the world of franchising. They typically have relationships and partnerships with numerous franchisors, and they can help you narrow down the options to find the best match for you.

And the best part? When you work with a reputable, trustworthy franchise coach, their services will often be free.

Wait a second … free? How is that possible?

Remember those partnerships that franchise coaches have with franchisors? Well, these coaches get a "finder's fee," so to speak, as compensation for helping a franchisor find its next stellar owner—kind of like recruiters in the corporate world. Franchisors are always on the lookout for new owners, and franchise coaches play a role in finding those people and helping the franchisors grow. Their interactions create a mutually beneficial relationship.

But back to you—you are probably overwhelmed by the franchise options out there. Maybe you are not sure where to start your search, what criteria to consider, and how to keep from pigeonholing yourself in one particular area. Your franchise coach (or advisor, consultant, or broker—we call ourselves by many different names) should be fully focused on you.

At FranCoach, for example, we work with so many franchisors that we can always honestly say that we do not care which franchise you start … our goal is simply to help you find YOUR best fit. If you do end up working with a franchise coach, make sure you pick one with numerous partnerships. That way, you can count on the fact that you will truly get the chance to find the franchise that is right for YOU.

At the end of the journey of finding your best franchise to own—we call this the "Discovery Process"—it will be so clear you have found your perfect match that you will not even be making a decision.

Seriously.

We say this to our clients all the time, and we know that they do not really believe us at the start. But when they get all the way to the end … it is either HECK YES, this is the right franchise for me (small point, but the franchise has to also say HECK YES, you are the right fit for them, too) or it is a clear no. You do not want to start a "maybe" franchise any more than you want to marry a "maybe" person (only my wife was allowed to marry the maybe person).

Doing your due diligence and conducting robust research will help you have the confidence to say HECK YES when you get to the end of the Discovery Process. That is where a franchise coach comes in … and, frankly, we cannot recommend using one enough.

---
CHAPTER 4
---

# The Best Franchises
# and Industries

## What Is the Best Franchise to Own?

Finding the right franchise for YOU all sounds well and good …
until you start wondering about the best franchise in the market or
the best industry to own a franchise in.

So what *is* the best franchise to own? What industry do you
*need* to stake a claim on?

The short answer is … there isn't one. Seriously! There is not
**one** best franchise or **one** best industry. There is not a hottest
industry or something you "must own." And anyone telling you
otherwise either doesn't know what they are talking about or is
trying to sell you something.

But how can that be? Isn't there one franchise brand that is
outperforming the others or one industry that is totally taking off
at the moment?

There are several reasons the whole "hottest" industry or brand
myth is, well … a myth.

First off, if there was only ONE best franchise, wouldn't everyone want to own it? But really, let's think through this a bit. We
have already established that finding the best franchise to own is

an incredibly individualized and personalized process. In fact, it is a process that **requires you to be selfish** so that you truly understand what you want to do every day as an owner. Given those facts, how could you possibly say any one franchise is the BEST?

You can't. The franchise that is best for YOU to own might be the worst possible option for your neighbor to own, and vice versa. After all, you did not marry their spouse—they did. You did not buy their house—they did. They are doing what is best for them while you are doing what is best for YOU. What is best for one person is not necessarily best for the next. The important piece is finding what is right for you, without worrying about what other people are doing.

Think back to the Get Out of Bed Test … being selfish and not falling for myths about the "hottest" industry or "best" brand is how you ensure that you find YOUR best franchise to own.

"Okay fine," you might be thinking. "But what about the cash? Isn't there a franchise in which the owners are making more than any other franchise owners? I want to get in on that!"

We're going to dive deeper into the financial side of franchising in Chapters 5 and 6, but keep this tidbit in mind … **The money follows the fit**.

Remember, the right franchise for YOU to own will be one that allows you to spend your days doing tasks you enjoy and are good at. So sure, there might be a franchise with owners who are rolling in it, so to speak. But let's say that a particular franchise requires owners who want to be the face of the business, who need to be out in the community shaking hands and kissing babies all day. If you hate people and would rather be holed up inside, working from your home office, you are not going to succeed with that franchise.

The franchise that will be the most lucrative for YOU is the one that lets your skill set shine and that makes you *excited* to get out of bed in the morning. Anything less will not allow you to realize your full potential. Again, **the money follows the fit.**

### What About That Article I Just Read on Google?

We suggest returning to the section entitled "Why Isn't Google Our Friend?"

Just kidding—stumbling upon a listicle or two during your search for the perfect franchise is inevitable. And in some cases, these articles can even be educational. The trick is knowing how to sift through the information to find out what applies to YOU.

(Have you noticed that we keep capitalizing the word "you"? That's because YOU are the most important factor in what franchise is the right match for your unique needs, goals, and priorities.)

Let's say you are scrolling on your phone and come upon a list or an article that talks about a specific franchise or industry. Should you ignore it? Or can you find something helpful there?

We will use the pet industry as an example. You might read an article that talks about how the pet industry is a $320 billion industry and mentions that 66 percent of U.S. households own a pet. The article also discusses how most pet owners (a whopping 97 percent) consider their animals to be part of the family ... and, in many cases, they like the pet more than their spouse or kids.

So you read this article and think, "Wow, this is the industry for me." And maybe it is! But maybe you think about it some more and realize that you do not really like dogs all that much. And the only thing you like less than dogs is dog owners. You start considering the types of customers you want to have, and you fear that the passion these owners will have for their pets may never allow you to truly make them happy. You worry there will be complaints and issues, and you feel that these customer relationships might be too personal. Maybe you would prefer a more transactional customer, after all.

Yes, that article made the pet industry sound amazing—and it can be. But that does not mean it has to be amazing for YOU.

When you read an industry spotlight article like this (as long as you read it with the right mindset), the benefit is that it can confirm what YOU want in your franchise ... and what you don't. In this example, the pet industry is not it.

You might also find a list somewhere with a title like "10 Top Franchises" or "Hottest Industry Trends." Again, go ahead and read it. But do so while keeping in mind that the search for the right franchise is all about YOU.

Sometimes, a list like this might open your eyes to something you never thought of or didn't even know existed. Even if that brand ends up not being the right option for you, it may still help point you in the right direction.

Maybe you read that article about the pet industry and, while it initially sounded great, you ultimately realized it would be too personal with customers for you. But then, what if you discovered that, within the pet industry, there was a franchise that specialized in picking up dog poop (yes, this seriously exists). The dog poop franchise could help you tap into the fact that 65.1 million households in the U.S. own a dog—but you can still maintain that less personal, more transactional business model that is right for you.

Google is not always your friend when it comes to finding the best franchise to own ... but that doesn't mean you can't find helpful information there. You just need to remember that the most important piece of information is YOU and what you want to do every day as an owner. There is no list or article that is going to tell you that.

## How Should I Interpret Trends in Franchising?

In addition to articles about individual franchise brands and industries, you might also see articles about top "trends" in a certain industry or in the franchising world as a whole. Like anything you find on the internet, the most important piece of the equation is learning how to read these articles through a critical (and selfish) lens.

Let's say there is a new article about the "hottest" or "trendiest" happenings in a certain industry. It might seem super exciting to learn about some new health and wellness trends, and the franchise options that go with them. No article or list or podcast is going to miss out on promoting fun buzzwords and statistics to make a topic look great and get lots of clicks.

I mean, can you imagine reading a dating profile that leads with "heavy snorer, loves professional wrestling, and lives in mom's basement"? Of course not. Just like your dating app matches, franchises (and the articles that spotlight them) are only going to advertise the good stuff.

So when you hear about the newest trends in health and wellness, it might sound exciting … but is it really? And more importantly, is it exciting for YOU?

Maybe it is! Maybe you love the fact that you could own a business on the front end of the wave in a new niche. Maybe you are excited to make an impact on the community with the brand-new "it" workout in wellness. Maybe you are thinking that, by being one of the early adopters in a brand, you could have the ability to influence the growth of the entire franchise in addition to your individual units. All of that could be true.

But on the flip side, maybe you learn that you are a bit more risk averse than that. Maybe you are skittish about a brand-new franchise in a brand-new industry. You might be more comfortable with a franchise that has more of a proven track record (for instance, one that has been in business for 20 years and has 400 owners). That long-standing franchise will have a ton of historical data on both the brand and the industry. You might also realize that the super cool new wellness brand is more of a want than a need for consumers, and that you are more comfortable with the prospect of a tried-and-true, need-based business.

Ultimately, there is no such thing as a "best" or "hottest" franchise or industry. There is, however, a best franchise for YOU— and that is what you need to focus on.

### Busting the Myth of the "Hottest" Industry

A few sections ago, we talked about how **you do not need specific industry experience to own a franchise**. We wanted to bring this topic up again as a quick reminder, because the allure of a so-called "hottest industry" can sometimes be hard to resist. So instead of worrying about what industry is trendy at the moment, let's just ditch the topic of "industry" altogether.

Believe it or not, when we work with clients at FranCoach, the industries someone is interested in or experienced in are some of the least important topics we discuss. Don't get me wrong—industry is still a factor, and we do talk about it. But it plays a much smaller role than many people think. Ultimately, it is very rarely the driver for finding your perfect franchise fit.

How is that possible? Remember, as a franchise owner, you are rarely the doer. That means that having years of experience in a given industry does not really matter—nor does having a "passion" for a certain industry.

However, once we determine a few industries that you are interested in, it can be helpful to dive deeper in order to compare and contrast. Let's say you are considering the newer, trendy wellness niches but are also attracted to home services, because you never see that niche going out of style. Looking at the similarities and differences between these two industries can help you get a better sense of which one best aligns with what you are looking for.

When you compare a few industries of interest and reflect on what is truly important to you, you will be one step closer to finding YOUR perfect franchise to own and to finally taking control over your personal and professional life.

## What Is the Franchise Discovery Process?

We have mentioned the "Discovery Process" a few times in this book as we discuss the path toward finding the right franchise for YOU. Now, let's take a closer look at what this phrase means and why it matters.

The **Discovery Process** describes all of the steps that take place while an individual vets a franchisor—and remember: The franchisor is vetting you as well. When done properly, this process typically spans six to eight weeks and can involve upward of 15 different steps. Here are a few of the steps that might be included …

### #1: Introduction to the Brand

When you work with a franchise advisor (again, we highly recommend this), that person will pair you with a few different franchises based on the information you have shared about your ideal owner role, what type of staff you want, your budget, and all the other information we have covered that contributes to determining YOUR perfect franchise.

Your franchise coach will introduce you to each brand, sharing some information about what it is all about and why they have chosen it for you. Then, you will get an introduction to a point person within the brand who will guide you through many of these steps. Usually, that person will have a title along the lines of "Director of Franchise Development."

### #2: Brand Overview

As you work with your franchisor liaison, you will begin gaining more information about the brand. You will get a high-level look at the brand, what products or services it provides, and who the customers are. You will also learn about the business model, location requirements, staff requirements, what the brand looks for in an owner, and the areas of support that you can expect from the franchisor.

These areas of support will include segments on things like sales, marketing, operations, technology, and so much more. It is relatively common for franchisors to break up all of this information into two or three calls (or sometimes webinars). It can be a bit overwhelming how much information comes at you, and fast! But remember, all of this information is going to help you gain a deeper understanding of whether or not a given brand is right for YOU.

### #3: Franchise Disclosure Document Review

**Franchise Disclosure Document**, or FDD, contains lots of information that the franchise is legally obligated to share with you per regulations regarding **responsible franchising**. Here are some of the sections you can expect to find there:

- A history of the company, including information about key officers

- Fees and costs, including royalties, transfer fees, renewal fees, and more
- Contractual obligations of both the franchisee and the franchisor
- Information about the **territory** you will receive
- Financial performance metrics for existing owners and company financial statements
- The **Franchise Agreement**
- And more …

Navigating all of this information probably sounds like a challenge—but guiding you through it is part of the job of your liaison who works for the franchisor.

### #4: Validation Calls

We will talk more about this topic in Chapter 10, but basically, **Validation Calls** give you the opportunity to discuss all that you have learned up to this point about a given franchise with its current franchisees. This helps you, you know … *validate* the information that you are hearing from the franchisor's own representative. After your point person with the franchise helps walk you through the FDD, they will help organize the Validation Calls.

Although you are getting a ton of information, remember that the franchisor is vetting you, too. In fact, everyone is …

The Validation Calls with the owners are certainly designed to help you learn more about the franchise, but the owners are checking you out at the same time. In fact, the owners on your Validation Calls can be the toughest on a candidate.

Why? Because this is THEIR brand. They do not want anyone coming into the franchise who might mess things up or be a "problem child," so to speak. Even if you will be located across the country from them, owners are very possessive of their brand and they will not be shy about expressing concerns about you back to the franchisor.

And guess what … when you are a franchise owner on the other end of a Validation Call, you will be doing the exact same thing!

Again, we will talk more about Validation Calls—including what questions to ask and how to get the most out of these conversations—in Chapter 10. But, for now, all you need to know is that Validation Calls give you the chance to get to know other owners and ask crucial questions to learn more about the brand you are vetting.

### #5: Funding

Unfortunately, owning a franchise is not free. But if you are working with a good franchise consultant, they can help you learn more about your funding options and pair you with reputable funding options. If not, the franchisor should be able to point you in the right direction—there are companies whose sole focus is franchise funding.

Trust us when we say that you have options—we are going to dive deeper into the specifics of funding in the following pages.

### #6: Meet the Team Day

There are a few different names for this final step in the process of determining the best franchise to own: Discovery Day, Meet the Team Day, and even Confirmation Day. For now, we will stick with Meet the Team Day. Why? Because it aptly describes what this step is all about.

You will take a trip to the franchise headquarters (either in person or virtually) and ... you guessed it ... **meet their team!** As we cover the final stages of the franchise ownership process toward the end of this book, we will go into more detail about what to expect from Meet the Team Day. For now, think of it as your opportunity to confirm your confidence in moving forward with a given brand.

---

**DEFINITION**

The **Discovery Process** is a multi-step endeavor that covers all of the steps you will take on your way to becoming a franchise owner. Typically, this process takes six to eight weeks and can include more than 15 steps. Some of the key steps include an introduction to the franchisor, brand overviews, FDD review, Validation Calls, funding exploration, and attending Meet the Team Day.

---

## CHAPTER 5

# The Cost of Franchise Ownership

### How Much Does Franchise Ownership Cost?

Let's talk about a subject that is probably top of mind: Money.

Perhaps owning a franchise sounds even better than it did when you first picked up this book. You have a better understanding of what is most important in finding the best franchise (Reminder: You!), and you also know what *not* to focus on. That's all well and good ... but it doesn't matter if you can't afford to own a franchise.

The range of what it costs to own a franchise is about as wide as you can possibly imagine. We use many analogies that compare owning a franchise to buying a house, and the cost is no exception. (Don't panic—we are talking about a starter home in Kansas, not a McMansion in Los Angeles!)

The first franchises that come to mind for most people are going to be the big ones ... McDonald's, Taco Bell, and other major retail-based franchises. These are what we refer to as "two-comma franchises"—in other words, there are two commas in their Total Investment figure (it exceeds $1 million). This level of investment not only rules most of us out, but also can downright scare people off from even exploring the possibility of franchising.

It's true that Taco Bell's Total Investment costs can exceed $2 million—but they are on the extremely high end of the spectrum. Purchasing a Taco Bell is the equivalent of buying that big house overlooking the ocean. Sure, that would be amazing, but it is out of most people's reach (right now, at least—we'll get to how this could be you down the road later in this book).

If Taco Bell is the high end, what is the low end? Back to our housing analogies … could you buy a cute little fixer-upper starter home? Let's put this house in a real estate market like Manhattan, Kansas rather than Manhattan, New York. Do you have the cash for the down payment, good enough credit to get a home loan, and maybe a little money left over to get some new curtains and pay for movers? **If so, you can own a franchise.**

There will be hundreds of franchise opportunities that fit this financial profile and multiple funding options through which you can make it happen. Now, will the down payment on a starter home buy you 14 Taco Bells tomorrow? It will not. But will it give you the opportunity to take control of your life by owning a franchise? It most certainly will.

Let's dig a little bit deeper into funding a franchise. In this section, we will explore "Total Investment" (a crucial figure in franchise ownership), as well as investment ranges, funding options, and more. Buckle up—this is where your dreams of franchise ownership start to become reality.

### What Is Total Investment?

Before we continue talking about how much it costs to own a franchise, we need to properly understand a very important phrase in franchising: Total Investment. In fact, this phrase is so important that if you ever speak with a franchise or consume any information about a franchise that does not discuss Total Investment ... run away as fast as you can!

Total Investment includes three key items ...

### #1: The Franchise Fee

What is a Franchise Fee? This is a fee you pay to the franchisor in return for the rights to their name, brand, training, support, and overall recipe for success. The Franchise Fee has a range, but typically, you will see a number amount between $40,000 and $60,000.

The Franchise Fee is typically paid in full when you sign the Franchise Agreement, and it is a one-time payment that covers the duration of the Franchise Agreement (typically 10 years).

The 10-year commitment associated with a Franchise Agreement does not mean that you HAVE to own the business for that long. You can sell it at any point you see fit. This commitment also does not mean that you cannot own the business for more than 10 years. At the end of the term of a Franchise Agreement, you can always renew, usually for a shorter term. At that point, you will pay a fraction of the Franchise Fee, usually 10 percent.

### #2: Start-up Costs

Your start-up costs are the costs of getting the business open on day one. This amount will include a variety of items. If your franchise requires a retail or office space, every dime that you spend to find, secure, and build out the space—and even turn on the utilities—is included here. Start-up costs encompass all of the things you need to simply set up your business. Think of marketing campaigns that begin 60 to 90 days before opening, any staff hired pre-opening, training costs, travel costs, equipment and supply costs, and more.

### #3: Three Months of Operating Capital

The third component of the "Total Investment" figure is three months' worth of operating capital. This should include the amount of money needed to pay all of the business-related bills for the first three months your franchise is open. In the FDD, which you legally must receive before signing with any franchise, franchisors are required to include an estimate of this amount.

But beware … some franchisors lowball this value to make the Total Investment seem lower than it really is. Even when franchisors *do* have an accurate number here, it is important to evaluate that number carefully. Their estimated three months of operating capital is based on what owners in that franchise system report. However, owners are not required to report these numbers—so, while you can get a good representation of the three-month costs, it may not be a truly representative sample.

It is also important to keep in mind that three months of operating capital does not mean that you will be at a break-even point in your business (in other words, you still may be putting your own money into the business). To better understand that timeline, you need to know what questions to ask to find out when owners in a particular franchise break even on average. This is another place that a franchise advisor can help—they will coach you on what questions to ask during the Discovery Process so that you have all of the necessary information that will make you confident in a given franchise opportunity.

| DEFINITION |
| --- |

**Total Investment** is a figure that includes (1) the Franchise Fee, (2) start-up costs, and (3) three months of operating capital for a particular franchise. The Total Investment can be found in the FDD for each franchise. This value is meant to give you a better picture of the true costs associated with opening a certain franchise business.

### How Can Total Investment Figures Help Me?

Now that you know what **Total Investment** means, it can help you in a few ways. First, let's go back to our friend Google. While this is not necessarily Google's fault ... not all information about franchises and their investment levels that you find online is accurate.

We once had a client come to us thinking they could own a well-known sandwich franchise for an investment of just $20,000. Owning this franchise will actually cost you closer to $500,000— but this client had seen an ad online saying, "Own a Sub Franchise —$20,000!"

The advertisement was not a total lie (the brand's Franchise Fee at the time was $20,000), but remember that the Franchise Fee is just one part of the Total Investment figure you need to consider. The ad totally disregarded start-up costs and three months of operating capital. Now, this ad was not placed by the franchise in question—it was placed by someone trying to "sell" a franchise. But when you know the importance of Total Investment, it's easy to see that this claim is nowhere near reality.

You will also see lists on the internet advertising "Top Franchises Under $100K" or some other arbitrary cutoff. Again, these lists are not always adhering to the Total Investment of a franchise, even though the numbers are reported in the FDD for every franchisor.

As an example, there was one "Top Franchises Under $100K" list that included a well-known food franchise with a Total Investment typically above $1million. How could this brand possibly make an affordable franchises list? Well, that food franchise does have an option for going into shared locations (think gas stations, food courts, etc.) and had one location in a shared space clock in at under $100,000.

But dig a little deeper, and you will discover that the brand in question does not allow you to own ONLY a shared location. Those locations are awarded only after an owner has opened several standalone locations first … as you can see, these lists are not always painting the full picture.

As always, it is crucial to proceed with caution when you are looking at ads online. When you have Total Investment on your mind, you have a strong jumping-off point to know what questions to ask and where to find the information you *really* need.

### What Investment Ranges Will I See?

Let's dig a little bit deeper into the investment ranges that you can expect to see as you look into becoming a franchise owner. These are all designed to be ballpark estimates, so keep in mind that there will be some examples of franchises that do not fall into the ranges below. However, this set of ranges will hopefully give you a better idea of the types of franchise that could align with your budget.

## *Restaurants*

Think of standalone restaurants here—buildings that are not connected to anything else other than that particular business. Examples of standalone restaurant franchises are McDonald's, Taco Bell, Pizza Hut, and the like. As a rule, these are your "two comma" investments. They are also going to take the longest to get open for business because you are typically building everything from scratch rather than retrofitting an existing structure.

For standalone restaurants, the cash required in addition to any funding options (coming up soon!) can easily exceed $500,000.

## *Strip Mall Locations*

While you might not realize it, strip malls are a haven for franchises. Food is the industry that people most often think of in this context, but pretty much anything else you see in a strip mall could also be a franchise. Think about …

- **Fitness:** Any type of gym or boutique fitness studio (yoga, pilates, etc.)
- **Wellness:** IV drips, sauna studios, or day spas
- **Beauty:** hair salons, eyelash studios, or waxing locations
- **Pets:** grooming, supplies, or training stores
- **Non-QSR (quick service restaurant) food:** ice cream, cookies, or juice
- **Other services:** mail or shipping.

Anything in the non-food category, when you are thinking of franchises located in strip malls, typically comes in under $500,000 as a Total Investment and can sometimes even be as low as $200,000.

## QSR/Fast Casual Franchises in Strip Malls

Of course, there are also food options in strip mall locations. QSR and fast-casual dining options are popular here, with offerings like sandwiches, pizza, Mexican, salad, Asian, and more.

In general, these fast-casual options will come to around $500,000 as a Total Investment. Anything in a strip mall will take from 6–12 months, on average, from the time you sign the Franchise Agreement until the time you are open for business.

Ideally, the pre-open marketing plan will have potential customers lining up outside your doors on day one—but, remember, you will rarely break even on month one, let alone day one. From a cash perspective, expect to need about $100,000 liquid for a strip-mall-type franchise and raise that number to a minimum of $150,000 if that franchise is food-related.

## Non-Retail Options

Non-retail franchise opportunities can be home-based or they might have a small facility: space in an office park, an office space, or a storage facility. While many people do not think of these businesses when they think of the term "franchise," there are as many (if not more) non-retail options than there are retail options. Some examples of non-retail franchises include:
- Senior care
- Business coaching
- Mobile versions of retail brands (mobile dog grooming vans, in-home personal trainers, food trucks, etc.)
- Home services (over 40 niches)
- And many more …

## *Home Service Franchises*

The home services world is massive in and of itself. The word "home" can easily be exchanged for "business"—basically, the franchise is going into a residence or place of business to provide some type of service. There are over 40 different niches of franchises encompassed in this category. For simplicity's sake, we will roll them into three buckets: enhance, maintain, and repair.

**Enhance:** These brands are going into the home or business to … you guessed it … *enhance* something. This enhancement could be as simple as a fresh coat of paint, or it might be a $40,000 bathroom remodel. These businesses tend to have one-time, infrequent customers who pay higher ticket prices.

**Maintain:** These brands are providing simple, staple tasks such as lawn care, pest control, cleaning, or pool maintenance. The services are usually recurring, membership-type models. If you perform the service well, you can gain a customer for life.

**Repair:** To put it simply, repair brands fix stuff. Projects could be urgent, like a broken air conditioner in July, plumbing or electrical issues, or water damage. They can also be less urgent: The leather seat in my boat is ripped and I need it fixed!

One thing that nearly all home services brands have in common is that, as an owner, you are NOT the doer. Again, you can be a slob and own a cleaning franchise. You are not the one cleaning the home. You can have no clue which end of the hammer to hold and still own a kitchen remodeling franchise. You do not have to know how to spell "plumber" to own a plumbing franchise. Regardless of your experience, any of these home services categories could be a match for you.

The other commonality between home services brands is that many of them do not require retail space and some do not require any space at all. If there are vehicles or equipment involved, owners will sometimes rent space at a storage facility as the base of operations. Occasionally, you will want a small office, usually in a business park or light industrial area.

So how much do home services franchises cost? Almost all of these brands have a Total Investment of under $250,000 and some can even come in as low as $100,000.

The time to get your (proverbial) doors open is also shorter. At times, these non-retail brands can be open for business in just 60–90 days. The pre-open marketing should set you up to have customers during week one, ideally on day one. While the time to break even with a home services franchise can oftentimes be less than retail options, it is rarely in the first month. The liquidity needed for a non-retail franchise is normally around $50,000, but it can be less.

## What Funding Options Are Available?

Now that you have a better understanding of what Total Investment means and why it is so important, plus some investment ranges for franchise options, you are probably wondering … where does the money actually come from?

There are five common funding methods in franchising. These can be used as standalone options and some of them can be combined. Let's take a simplistic look at each of these five funding methods.

### 1. SBA Loan

An SBA Loan, or Small Business Association Loan, is the most common funding method used to own a franchise. However, it can also be the most cumbersome. Let's bring our housing analogy back into play to gain a better understanding of how the SBA Loan works.

Using an SBA loan is like getting a loan to buy a house. You need cash out of your pocket in order to get an SBA Loan, and then you need some money left over. So how much money can you get?

The range for an SBA Loan can be as low as $100,000, and it can go up to $5 million. Depending on a few factors, the cash required can vary, but a good estimate is about 30 percent of the loan amount. This combines the upfront cash out of pocket (like your down payment when buying a house) as well as the "cash reserves" for when you start your franchise (like having money left over for the movers and some new curtains when you buy a house).

The SBA Loan is a government-backed loan, but the government is not directly giving you the money. There are numerous requirements to qualify for the SBA Loan. While these can be initiated at your local bank, it is rare that your local branch has the understanding and bandwidth to do so. Instead, it is more typical to work with companies specifically dedicated to this loan process—and the majority of the money loaned out is from banks you have probably not heard of.

The additional requirements and terms for an SBA Loan can vary. At the time of this book's publication, we recommend that people have a credit score of at least 680 (over 700 is preferable). Interest rates vary based on prime.

One aspect where the SBA Loan differs from buying a home is time. It can take 60–90 days for an SBA Loan to close, and there are certain requirements that need to be met when the loan is used for a franchise, such as …

- You must have a signed Franchise Agreement.
- You must have completed your franchisor training.
- If there is a physical space, it must be ready to be occupied.

When we talk about the liquidity needed for a franchise, these factors can come into play if you are looking at a retail franchise. If your sole funding option is the SBA Loan, you might actually need more than 30 percent of your cash to come out of pocket, because you will need to invest in building your physical space before you get the loan.

### ROBS (Rollovers as Business Start-up) Program

The ROBS program is perhaps the least-known funding option, but it is also one that is very popular. Without getting too technical, the program allows you to take any or all of your money in a qualified retirement plan, typically a 401(k), and have it "roll over" to a new 401(k) account that is specifically set up for your business.

This transfer of funds is not penalized or taxed like it would be when the money is simply withdrawn. Once the funds are in the new 401(k) account, you can use it to fund all or part of your new franchise.

There are companies out there with the sole purpose of helping set up and manage this process. Don't worry that you have not heard of them. When you work with a franchise or a franchise advisor, they will have these partnerships ready for you.

The ROBS program can be used as the sole funding option for a franchise or it can be combined with another option. A very common combination we have seen is using both the ROBS program and the SBA Loan. Clients will use the ROBS for the liquidity to get open and the SBA Loan for the operating capital needed once the business is already open.

The ROBS option tends to provoke varied responses from potential franchisees. Some will look at the program as an amazing option. They see the ability to use their own money to fund a business and essentially diversify their portfolio. Those who are attracted to the ROBS also like the control aspect—they trust themselves to grow their own money as a franchise owner more than they trust the stock market to return 6 to 8 percent while their money sits in a 401(k).

## *HELOC*

The HELOC, or "home equity line of credit," is similar to the ROBS in that it allows people to use their own money versus taking out a true loan, like the SBA option. A HELOC provides the opportunity for people to tap into the equity they have amassed in their real estate. Plus, the process of accessing the money for a HELOC is significantly faster and can provide significantly lower interest rates than you would see with an SBA Loan.

The downside, from some perspectives, is that your house or real estate holdings are now tied to your franchise. Also, while your franchise coach or franchisor can connect you with industry leaders who have expertise in the SBA Loan and ROBS Program, the HELOC is typically something you have to figure out on your own as a potential franchisee.

## *Non-SBA Loan*

Yes, there are other types of loans you can access besides the SBA loans! Essentially, you will see term loan options and occasionally business lines of credit that might be available to you. The term loans can be a strong option because they can be funded within one to two weeks, as opposed to the months it takes for an SBA Loan to fund. There is often no cash required, and these are in no way tied to the franchise.

The flip side is that term loans are like hard money loans in real estate. The money is being loaned to you with no cash or collateral, so the catch is that the cost of the money in fees or interest rates may be higher. For some, the increase in fees or interest is worth it to be able to hold onto their cash—or maybe they lack the cash requirements for the SBA Loan and this is the only path. Others, however, prefer to use the SBA Loan and do not mind the cash out of pocket and the 90-day funding timeline, which is on the longer side, and the longer timeline for the loan to fund.

### Cash

Just like buying a house, some people simply pay cash. It is not an option for everyone, but it does happen —and the same is possible with a franchise. While paying cash is much less common, cash payers like the fact that they are putting their cash to work for themselves as a true, controllable investment instead of just letting it sit in a bank account somewhere.

## CHAPTER 6

# Earning Money as a Franchise Owner

## How Much Money Can I Make?

With the investment ranges and funding options for owning a franchise coming into focus, let's get down to the real money question ... how much can I make?

In short, you can make however much you want to make.

No, really—however much you want.

After all, why not? You are the boss. Your franchise will be however successful you want it to be based on your efforts and goals. There is no one holding you back. There is no glass ceiling on your earnings. There is no cap on your annual raise, and no performance reviews holding you back.

Being a franchise owner is about being in control. Remember, the number one reason people own a franchise is just that ... CONTROL. Most of the time, the main thing that people want to control is their lifestyle. Time, freedom, flexibility, all of that good stuff. We all need to eat and pay bills, so the money is not far behind—but the money is still about control. You want control over your talents and efforts being rewarded in the way you deserve.

In this chapter, we will take a look at the ways you can maximize the money you make as a franchise owner. We will also talk about how, when you find your happy place as a franchise owner (i.e., when you are spending the amount of time you want on your work and making the amount of money you want), you can settle in right there without anyone pushing you for more.

But first, let's talk about the most important factor on the money side of the equation. We'll also touch on how to avoid comparing your corporate salary to your compensation as an owner, which is like comparing … apples to pizza.

## How Do I Make More Money?

The money follows the fit.

Let's all say that again, together now: "The money follows the fit."

As we discussed earlier in this book, there is not one single "best" or "hottest" franchise—and, similarly, there is not one and only one franchise that will allow you to make however much money it is that you want to make.

Let's say your goal is to make $100,000 per year as a franchise owner. You come to FranCoach for support, looking for the right franchise, and you ask us, "Hey, what franchise is out there that will allow me to make $100,000 per year?"

Unfortunately, our answer is probably going to annoy you. We will tell you the truth: any of them.

How can this be possible? Again, **the money follows the fit**.

We will use the example of a senior care franchise. Let's say you are looking at a franchise in senior care. You hear from a few owners that, after a couple of years in business, their revenue is well into the seven-figure range, most of which is recurring and increasing. This looks like a lot of growth from an initial Total Investment of under $200,000.

Sounds amazing, right? You probably hear all of that and say, "Great, sign me up!" But what about the fit? What if, as an owner, you really do not like longer-term, repeat clients and are actually more comfortable with a project-based business? What if you do not want to have a big team, which is something that you definitely need in the in-home senior care space? What if, when you are honest with yourself, you remember that you do not really like old people?

Okay, fine, but still—those senior care franchise owners are making so much money! It seems almost irresistible. Well … resist.

The truth is, you will not ever make what they make because senior care sounds like a terrible fit for you. Plus, you are likely to be very unhappy day in and day out as a senior care franchise owner. If you want to wake up to something you do not enjoy doing, then just keep your current job.

This is why we say that the money follows the fit. And the flip side is also true—envision that the characteristics of an ideal senior care franchise owner align with your own strengths and interests. Maybe, dare we say it, senior care and helping elderly people in your community are even things you are "passionate" about. If all of that is true, then you have a great chance of meeting or even exceeding the numbers the other owners in that franchise system are earning.

## How Does Compensation Work?

The longer someone has been in the corporate world, the more likely they are to say something to the effect of: "If I own a franchise, I need to replace my salary of X from my current job."

Well … no. Actually, you don't. Yes, you need to have money to eat and to pay bills. But the corporate salary you have is not at all the same as how you compensate yourself as an owner—not even close. **In fact, what you actually need to replace is around half of your current salary.**

As an example, let's say that our client Bob has a job that pays him $150,000 annually. That sounds awesome for Bob but, in reality, he only sees around $100,000 of that, maybe $105,000 after taxes. Then, with what's left, Bob takes that money and pays all of his bills. Among these bills are things like his car payment, car insurance, and gas for the vehicle. He is also paying for his cellphone, his mortgage, and all of the utilities for his home. Bob's paycheck also bought him that really nice shirt that he wore to work today … don't worry Bob, that shirt will eventually come back into style.

As a franchise owner, Bob will still have all those bills to take care of … but he does not need to pay for them out of his pocket. Bob's franchise pays for them. The car is a business car. It probably has a wrap or something that showcases the name of the franchise and is thus paid for out of the business account rather than Bob's personal account. The same goes for the gas, maintenance, and insurance for the business vehicle.

Bob's cell phone is actually his business cell phone—and the same is true for the internet in his home office. In fact, a portion of Bob's mortgage and utilities are also technically now business expenses. And that plaid shirt with a butterfly collar that Bob was wearing to work is now replaced by a good-looking polo with the logo of his franchise on it, which was paid for by … wait for it … Bob's business!

All of those things that Bob used to pay for out of his own pocket from his $150,000 per year salary are now all part of the

Total Investment for his new franchise, thus lowering the amount of money that he needs to take home each month in order to live the life he wants.

If you have ever heard a business owner talk about a "write off," this is what they mean. Any expense that you paid for out of your pocket when you worked for someone else is now paid for by your business (as long as it touches your business in some way, of course). Printer ink, lunch with a business colleague, a new laptop … our friend Bob can now pay for all of these things through his business.

Now, I am not a Certified Public Accountant (CPA), but I will say this: Every business expense helps reduce the amount of tax that your business owes. So not only do these business expenses not come out of your own personal pocket, but there can also be tax savings.

When you start to add all of these things up, it becomes clearer how half of someone's corporate salary might be more than enough.

Comparing your corporate salary to your compensation as a franchise owner is, as I like to say, comparing apples to pizza. They are simply two entirely different compensation structures, so it is crucial not to get caught up in a vanity number here.

### How Do I Calculate the Financial Potential?

At this point, we have established a couple of things. First off, the money follows the fit. Finding the franchise that is right for YOU will maximize your earning potential as a franchise owner. Second, comparing your corporate salary to your compensation as a franchisor does not make much sense … just like comparing apples to pizza.

But you are probably still wondering how we can determine the financial potential in a franchise. It is the right question to be asking, but the answer is not always easy. Remember, this is not a job—there is no guarantee of what you will make. (And remember, too, that in a traditional job there is no guarantee on how long your employer will keep you as an employee!)

So how *do* we find out the financial potential of a certain franchise?

The FDD is a starting point. This document includes what is called an "Item 19," which is one of the first parts people tend to read. Why? This section has the revenue as reported by the brand's franchise owners. Franchisors are not required to include anything in this section, but most have at least something. However, the figures listed in Item 19 are not always easy to understand, nor do they paint the complete picture.

Item 19s tend to have ranges and averages, and they also typically organize data by the time an owner has been in business. Franchisees are not required to submit this information and franchisors are not required to display every owner's response. As you can see, while Item 19 seems like it would be super helpful, it is often anything but.

That said, there can be good data in this section of the FDD. For instance, you might find out that, after three years in business, owners have an average revenue of $1,000,000. You may read that the brand's top owner's revenue was $9,848,310 and the lowest earner brought in $451,993. Those are just two examples, but they illustrate how Item 19 can offer a starting point, but rarely provides the full or final picture.

With that in mind …

## How Do We Get a Clearer Picture of Financials?

In short, the answer is Validation Calls.

When you work with a franchise advisor like FranCoach, you will embark on a six-to-eight-week process of vetting franchisors—and they are vetting you, too—called the Discovery Process. Validation Calls are one step in that process.

These calls typically take place during the second half of the Discovery Process, and they give you the chance to talk to current franchise owners in a given brand. The calls can be the most informative and "real" part of the process. Of course, it is important to have smart, targeted questions to ask these owners in order to get the most out of your Validation Calls.

There will be many non-financial questions to ask but in this section, we will focus on questions related to money.

Rather than asking an owner, "Uh ... how much money do you make?" (a question that will make you look a little silly, by the way), it is best to ask specific questions to understand the costs and fees owners handle on a monthly basis.

For instance, you might ask them how much it costs to run the business each month at a high level. You could also dig deeper into how much they spend on marketing each month. Each of these are much better questions and will help you gather a much more complete picture of the financials behind owning that specific franchise.

The same logic applies to revenue. To determine how much money an owner is bringing in, you could simply ask them how much revenue they average per month. That is not the worst question. But what if you asked a more granular question that helps you figure out how they get there?

Let's say there is a painting franchise owner, Shannon, making $50,000 in revenue per month. She was kind enough to share that one piece of information—but, if she tells us the business averages $5,000 per transaction, we have an even better way to actually project the revenue.

## What About Net Profit?

Another way to get confused—or, worse yet, get poor information—is focusing on the "net profit" of a particular band. Franchisors will throw that phrase around relatively often. They do not always mean for it to be misleading ... but it is. Why?

Remember back in the day, in math class, when you would give an answer (even a correct answer!) and get in trouble? Why did that happen? Because you did not show your work.

I like to equate net profit to an answer without showing us any work to support it. As a potential franchise owner, you HAVE to see the "work" behind that number. Otherwise, you are setting yourself up for potential financial disappointment.

It is crucial to understand the revenue model rather than just the bottom-line number. It is okay to know that the average owner of a certain brand brings in $50,000 per month in revenue. But how did they get there?

Let's say we are talking about a painting franchise. We can get some more information about the average ticket price. If we know that the average project yields $5,000, then we know that equates to about 10 jobs per month.

Questions like this will give us a much better idea of *how* the revenue works, not just *what* the number is. Imagine that you talk to an owner who tells you it costs $30,000 per month to run the business minus any owner compensation, and the business brings in an average of $50,000 per month. With that information, you know that the business has a gross profit of $20,000 per month. Then, subtract all of the things that you as an owner will have your business pay for: car, phone, computer, etc. Let's say that adds up to $5,000 per month, leaving the business with $15,000 per month.

What do you do with this money? You are the owner—do whatever you want with it! If you want to take half of that and pay yourself a salary, go ahead. If so, that $7,500 plus the equivalent of $5,000 of expenses you are running through the business means you are taking home the equivalent of $12,500 per month ... which is more than you would see with your $150,000 per year corporate salary!

What else can you do with this money? Some owners, believe it or not, pay themselves little to nothing from their business. Why? Usually because they have a spouse who is earning money as well and that is how they pay for their personal expenses. You could also take every dime out of the business and jet off to Tahiti for a month with your spouse. That might not be the smartest business decision ever—but it is YOUR business, so do what you want!

The smart franchise owner will keep some money in reserve while also looking at ways to reinvest in the business for growth. Maybe it is time for more marketing, another truck, a new employee ... or maybe you are ready for a new franchise location. You wanted control. Now, you have it!

### What Is My Exit Strategy?

At this point, you have a handle on the money that you can earn as a franchise owner. You also know how to properly calculate those potential earnings and understand how there is no ceiling on the amount of money you can make.

Now, it is time to talk about the final piece of the financial puzzle: your exit strategy.

Like most things in franchising, an exit strategy as a franchise owner is totally different from that of a corporate employee.

As an employee, when you leave your job (whether it is your choice or your boss's choice), the financial element of employment is over. Your paycheck stops. You do not get to sell your job to the next person, nor do you get to pass it on to someone in your family.

As a franchise owner, you *can* do either one of those things! So make all the money you want as a franchise owner for as long as you want. When you do not want to own the business anymore … sell it and cash out.

These are some of the hidden beauties of franchise ownership—the equity you build and the ability to create generational wealth for your family. And remember, those are two things you cannot do as an employee.

## CHAPTER 7

# How Franchise Ownership Supports YOU

## Why Do I Have to Pay a Franchise Fee?

When we explored the concept of Total Investment in the previous section, we mentioned the Franchise Fee. When you sign a Franchise Agreement, you pay a Franchise Fee. These fees range somewhere between $40,000 and $60,000 for most franchise opportunities.

However, these fees can sometimes cause people to wonder, "Why can't I just do this myself?"

Maybe you can—and maybe you should. But most people are not willing to take on the incredible risk of pioneering a business from scratch. So if you *are* paying a Franchise Fee, you are probably wondering what you are getting in exchange.

In short ... how does the Franchise Fee benefit YOU?

First and foremost, you are paying for the right to own the brand ... the logo, the trademark, the recipe for success, and the support to make it happen. Franchises are NOT sold—they are awarded. At times, people talk to a franchise and think that the franchise is trying to "sell" them on the brand. They are not. Yes, it is their job to highlight the virtues of their franchises ... but they are also vetting *you* to ensure that you are the right fit for them. This Discovery Process is very much like dating—the attraction has to be mutual before anyone says, "I do."

Once the franchise is awarded, the Franchise Agreement is signed, and the Franchise Fee is paid … you are an owner! But what are you getting for that money?

Basically, the franchise is going to support you in countless ways. In a couple of sections, we are going to take a deep dive (yep, there is a case study and everything!) into the differences between owning a franchise and starting a business from scratch. But first, let's talk a little bit more about the Franchise Fee and why you need to pay it.

There is a common misconception that the franchisor is making money from your Franchise Fee. The reality is quite the opposite.

Let's say that your Franchise Fee is $50,000. What does that cover?

First off, there are a number of costs that the franchise incurs before you even become an owner. Your Franchise Fee will help pay for the salaries of the support team at the franchise who helped you out during your journey to become a franchise owner. There are also numerous people working for the franchise who will help train and onboard you, support you as you open for business, and travel to your location as you are getting up and running. All of those people need to be paid, too. Basically, the Franchise Fee covers a small portion of the money the franchisor is investing in you until they start collecting **royalties**.

The franchise is making an investment in you before you even get going, all in the hopes that you are a good owner and they will eventually start seeing the royalty dollars come in. This is why the franchisor is *vetting* you, not *selling* you a franchise.

It also takes an incredible investment of both time and money (seriously, hundreds of thousands of dollars) for a business to become a franchise. And that is not even considering the time and money needed to sustain the business until it is self-sufficient based on royalties.

Now, does anyone who is thinking about becoming a franchise owner really care about this? Not really. But hopefully, it helps to drive home how insignificant that $50,000 Franchise Fee really is to the franchisor and why they go to such great lengths to vet you to ensure that you are the right fit for their brand.

### How Often Do I Pay the Franchise Fee?

You will pay the Franchise Fee once, and it is good for the lifetime of the agreement. Most Franchise Agreements span 10 years. There are some that are a little shorter and some that are a little longer.

But wait ... does that mean you are locked into that agreement for 10 YEARS?

Not really. The ultimate exit strategy is always to sell your franchise when you are finished running it. The wealth and equity you build is such a huge component of why people want to own a franchise. If you want to sell your franchise before the end of the Franchise Agreement, you can absolutely do so. No one is stopping you. Therefore, you are not really locked in for the entire duration of the agreement.

But what if you want to continue owning the franchise once the term of your Franchise Agreement ends? Well, you can renew it!

If you are a franchisee in good standing, the franchisor will offer you a renewal agreement. This renewal agreement usually covers a shorter period of time. You will pay a Franchise Fee for the renewal, but it is a fraction of the original fee. Often, the renewal fee can be as low as 10 percent of the original Franchise Fee.

## Why Do I Have to Pay Royalties?

Now that you know more about the Franchise Fee, let's talk about those pesky royalties. When it comes to franchise ownership, "royalties" can be a scary word—people are often deterred by the concept of royalties. But when we break down this concept, it is clear why they are important (and necessary).

### What Is a Royalty Fee?

A royalty is the fee that a franchise owner pays to the franchisor. It is a percentage of the gross revenue (typically somewhere between 4 percent and 12 percent) and it is paid on a regular basis for the entirety of the time you own the franchise. Normally, you will pay royalties monthly, but sometimes this cadence can be more frequent.

### Why Do I Have to Pay Royalties?

"Wait," you are probably thinking … "So you are telling me that I have to give a percentage of my hard-earned money to the franchisor every month for the entire time that I own the franchise. Why?"

That is a great question, and there are two main reasons.

## #1: Royalties Are How the
## Franchisor Makes Money

The franchisors are business owners too—and, as a business owner, it is your right and your goal to make money. After all, the franchisor created the entire business model, investing hundreds of thousands of dollars to turn it into a franchise and build an entire team dedicated to supporting you and your fellow franchisees. In turn, they deserve to make money, and royalties are how they do so.

But that is only a portion of where the royalty dollars go. They also help you as a franchise owner. How?

## #2: Royalties Go Back Into
## the Business to Help It Grow

As a franchise owner, every dollar that your business has in the bank (after paying your monthly bills, of course) is yours to do with what you wish. If you have $50,000 left over at the end of the month and you want to pull out every dime to take a tropical vacation with your spouse ... do it. It is YOUR money.

Now, is that the smartest way to spend your money? Probably not. As an owner, what you *should* do with that money is set some aside for a rainy day and then take some to reinvest in your business. Perhaps you decide to increase your marketing efforts, maybe you need a new vehicle for your plumbing franchise, or maybe you want to expand your staff. Maybe you are ready to add a second location. Either way, you are putting YOUR money toward growth.

The same applies to the franchisor. Part of the royalty money the franchisor collects is reinvested back into the business, which means growing YOUR business. The partnership between a franchisor and a franchisee should always be a win-win. The better a franchisor does with training and support, the better their owners do with running their businesses. The better the owners run their businesses, the more royalty dollars they pay and the better the franchisor does.

You have probably heard the expression, "Happy wife, happy life." In the franchising world, we like to say, "Happy franchisees, happy franchisors."

## DEFINITION

**Royalties** are ones of the fees that you pay to the franchisor as a franchise owner. They are typically collected on a monthly basis and range from 4 percent to 12 percent of gross revenue. Royalties are where the franchisor makes their money, not the Franchise Fee. Franchisors use the royalty money to build infrastructure that supports you as an owner and helps you succeed. Royalties are a part of a mutually beneficial franchisee–franchisor relationship that allows both parties to grow their businesses and experience continued success.

### What Do Franchisors Use Royalty Money For?

Are you wondering what franchisors spend those royalty dollars on? Let's take a closer look—and remember, these fees are intended to benefit both you *and* the franchisor.

For instance, most franchisors will have a business coach who is there to support their owners. That business coach, who is paid for by the royalty dollars, can help with any and all aspects of running a franchise unit. Perhaps they will provide you with advice on understanding the marketing metrics, ensure efficiency with ordering or inventory, or even provide support related to hiring and retaining staff.

The franchisor may also use the royalty money to pay their team that is working on negotiating better rates on products for your business—think wholesale napkin discounts, national accounts to acquire customers, and the like. Maybe they are using royalties to invest in new software or technology, like finding a creative way to use artificial intelligence to stay ahead of the competition.

Again, the better you do and the happier you are as a franchisee, the better the franchisor does—and, really, the better the entire system does.

One question that we often like to have our clients ask the franchisor toward the end of the Discovery Process is, "What exactly do I get for the royalties I pay?"

When you ask this of a franchisor, you will get one of two responses. Either they will say, "We take your royalties and go to Tahiti once a month," or their answer is going to be really long and outline all of the ways in which the royalty money goes toward supporting you and helping you grow as a franchise owner. (Hint: You will get the second answer.)

## Why Would I Start a Franchise Instead of Building a Business From Scratch?

When it comes to franchise ownership, the word "royalties" sometimes scares people away. People think, "Why can't I just start a business from scratch and not have to pay the Franchise Fee and royalties?"

Well, of course you can. Maybe that *is* the best path for you to go down. Who knows—perhaps you start your business and it goes so well that you end up turning it into a franchise. After all, that is how franchisors come to be.

So why would starting your own business be a better path for you than owning a franchise? If this sounds like you, then you might be well-suited for starting something from scratch. For example:

- You refuse to follow other people's plans.
- You love the challenge of starting something from nothing.
- You enjoy the trial and error of figuring everything out for yourself and hoping it works (and fixing all of the things that don't work before it is too late).
- You are more of a pioneer, go-it-alone type of person.

If those statements resonate with you, then a franchise might not be the right fit. But for everyone else, that probably sounds incredibly risky. And it is.

The failure rate of non-franchise businesses is high for many, many reasons. In fact, 45 percent of small businesses fail within the first five years. But, for some, starting from scratch is the best option.

We often get asked, "Why should I open a franchise instead of starting something myself?"

My answer is always, "Franchise ownership might not be the right path for you ... but the list of reasons it might be is long."

Let's work through an example—we will call our business "Tim's Sandwich Shop."

## CASE STUDY: TIM'S SANDWICH SHOP

I make a killer peanut butter and jelly sandwich, and my ham and cheese sandwich is no slouch either. So I have decided to start my own sandwich business. Sure, I could just find a sandwich franchise, but I am confident that I can do this all on my own way better and way cheaper than that sandwich franchise everyone loves.

First off, I am going to need a logo for Tim's Sandwich Shop. Who can make a good logo? What does a good logo even look like? How do I know it will resonate and send the right message to potential customers? How much will it cost me?

Oh, wait ... I should probably trademark the name and then the logo. How does this work? How long does it take? (Hint: The trademarking process is not quick.) Who can help me out with this process and how much will it cost?

Next up, I am definitely going to need a website. What should it look like? What information should I put on it? I am not a website designer, so who should I hire to do it for me? How much will *that* cost?

If someone Googles "sandwich shop near me," will they see my website? How do I get Tim's Sandwich Shop to the top of Google? How much will it cost to rank above Subway, Jimmy John's, Jersey Mike's Firehouse Subs, and every other big-name sandwich franchise? (Hint: So much more than you can imagine!)

If that sounds like a lot to consider ... it is. But we're just getting started!

There are so many other questions to think about when you look at starting your own business ...
• Where should my location be?
• How do I find the best location?
• How do I know it is a good location, since I have never owned a retail business before?
• How do I negotiate the lease? (Hint: You should never pay the retail price for a retail location.)
• What is a T.I. or triple net lease?
• How do I source the right contractors to build out my location?
• How do I know what the best build-out options are?
• And of course ... how much will all of this cost?

Let's assume that you make it past all those pressing (and expensive) concerns about location. Now what?

Well, Tim's Sandwich Shop needs napkins. Where do I buy those? How do I know if they are good napkins? Am I getting a good price for the napkins? Now, replicate those questions for every other product you need in the store.

Next up, we are going to have to hire some people. What does the job description need to look like for my sandwich artist? How do I train the staff to cut the tomatoes properly and ensure that they do it the same way every single time?

(Hint: All these are topics the franchisor will have in place as part of their plan.)

You get the idea—when you are starting a business from scratch, there are about a million questions to consider. So how is that different as a franchise owner?

## How Does a Franchise Simplify the Process of Opening a Business?

To put it simply, the franchisor has a proven plan in place for every last detail of the business ...

A trademarked name and logo? Check.

A proven marketing plan to get the business listed at the top of Google search results, not to mention a full marketing plan and content in place for every possible marketing avenue you might want to pursue? Check.

A real estate team to help you find and negotiate all aspects of the retail location? Check.

A full training program for every single person you ever hire, plus job descriptions that are ready to go, guidance on where to post them, and even support making final hiring decisions? Yep, they have got that, too.

Remember the napkin situation? The franchise will not only tell you which ones to buy, but also give you access to buy them at a huge discount because the franchisor will have negotiated a lower rate due to the purchasing power they have as an entire franchise system as opposed to just one person. In other words ... napkins? Check.

What about training? In addition to a training program for your employees, *you* will also receive training on every single aspect of running a business in general—but also all of the specifics of that particular franchise. This includes ongoing training and support, which usually involves an actual business coach.

BECOMING A FRANCHISE OWNER

In reality, an entire book could be written detailing all of the support systems that franchises have laid out and have proven successful. This is why franchisees have a significantly higher success rate as business owners than true start-ups. In fact, with all of these assets on your side, it can be hard to fathom why someone would struggle or fail as a franchise owner.

## CHAPTER 8

# Franchising as a Side Gig

### Can I Keep My Job and Start a Franchise?

Yes.

This is what is commonly referred to as being a "semi-absentee owner."

This term is a fancy way of saying that your role as an owner is part-time. The business, of course, still runs full-time. Most semi-absentee owners have another commitment that occupies their time—typically, they are keeping their corporate job *and* owning the franchise. Some people own multiple businesses and take on semi-absentee roles in all of them. Others are semi-retired and working part-time as a semi-absentee franchise owner.

So what does semi-absentee ownership look like ... and could it be the right path for you?

### What Is Semi-Absentee Franchise Ownership?

There are many aspects to understand if you are considering semi-absentee franchise ownership. First, "semi-absentee" is the most poorly defined term in franchising. If you ask 10 franchisors to define it, you will likely get 15 different answers.

Second, not every franchise is open to semi-absentee own-ers. These differences are not industry-specific either. You could find two franchises that do the exact same thing … one of them could love semi-absentee owners and the next might require every owner to be full time.

Even when franchises *are* open to semi-absentee owners, there are usually major differences in what that means between each fran-chise. One might say that a semi-absentee owner must commit to 10 hours per week. The next franchise may say that semi-absentee own-ership requires 20 to 25 hours per week. Again, this can happen with two franchises in the same industry that do the exact same thing.

You might also run into a franchise that says they are open to semi-absentee owners but do not really have any experience with that model. There are other brands that really focus on semi-ab-sentee owners and others still that have a 50/50 split between semi-absentee and full-time owners. As you can see, brands run the full spectrum.

Making this even more confusing is our frenemy, Google. Information about semi-absentee ownership is not something that you can typically find through an internet search.

In that case, how can you find out which franchise is which? Well, that is where a franchise coach (like a member of our team at FranCoach) comes into play. To be honest, without expert guid-ance from someone with a deep understanding of the franchising space, it is virtually impossible to know without literally talking to every single franchise you think you might be interested in.

Now you know two things: (1) it is possible to keep your job AND become a franchise owner, and (2) there are many variables in the realm of semi-absentee ownership.

Let's go back to what is always the most important factor in this process: YOU.

**DEFINITION**

**Semi-absentee ownership** is a fancy way of saying that your role as a franchise owner is part-time. While your business will still run full-time, you may have another job or commitment that means you only work on that business for a limited number of hours per week. Typically, the job of a semi-absentee owner is managing the full-time manager who runs the day-to-day operations of the business. What semi-absentee ownership looks like can differ greatly from one franchise to the next.

## Is Semi-Absentee Ownership Right for Me?

How do you know if YOU are cut out for being a semi-absentee franchise owner? There are a few things to think about.

First, how big of a control freak are you? Do you always have to make every single decision, regardless of how big or small it is? Can you delegate, or are you a micromanager? Can you multitask? Do you REALLY have the time to commit to the franchise? And, more importantly, WILL you commit that time?

As a semi-absentee owner, your main role will be managing the manager who runs the day-to-day operations of your franchise. **If you are not comfortable with this, then semi-absentee ownership is not for you.**

If it still sounds like a possibility, there are a few factors to look at ...

### *Consideration #1: Time*

When our team at FranCoach talks to clients about semi-absentee ownership, one of the biggest things we discuss is time. How much time during the week can you dedicate to your franchise? This does not mean being physically present at the location (if there is one)—it just means that, if you say that every day from 8 a.m. to 9 a.m. you are going to focus ONLY on your franchise, can you *really* do that?

Again, most of this time can be remote. Semi-absentee ownership could look like checking on sales metrics on your laptop while sitting on your couch in the evening or ordering supplies while you sip coffee on your patio on a Saturday morning. But either way, you have to put in the required amount of effort.

At minimum, I would say that an aspiring semi-absentee franchise owner should be able to dedicate 10 hours per week to the franchise. Again, much (and sometimes all) of this can be remote. Remember, some franchises may require more time out of their semi-absentee owners (although some may require a little less).

### *Consideration #2: Owner Role*

After we get a handle on the amount of time per week someone can honestly commit, then we need to think about what you want to do. Just like an owner who will be full-time in their franchise, you also need to think about the Get Out of Bed Test.

Maybe you really love connecting in the community and networking. Well, some of your 10 hours per week might be spent getting out there and doing that type of work for your franchise. On the other hand, maybe that sounds awful—and in that case, you might hire a general manager who *is* good at networking.

Maybe you are more operations-driven, so much of your time will be focused on general oversight of the business and keeping a close eye on the financials.

It does not matter what you want to do as an owner … you are the boss. But it is crucial to be honest with yourself about what you want to do (and enjoy doing) and what you don't. Do what you do best and hire for the rest!

### Consideration #3: Accessibility

The third factor to think about is your accessibility. You will hire a manager, but if they need you, how quickly can you reply? If your general manager calls you at 10 a.m. on a Tuesday, how often will you be able to answer the phone? If you cannot pick up, how long will it take you to shoot them a text? An hour? A day? A week?

It does not matter what the answer is, as long as it is honest. The crucial thing here is to make sure that proper expectations are set for everyone involved.

While most people could reply to a call, text, email, or Slack message within an hour or two, we have worked with a few clients who cannot always be that responsive. For instance, we had a client who was an airline pilot and became a semi-absentee franchise owner. I really want to believe that he was not up there in the cockpit flying the plane while making calls and texting people about his franchise.

While he was working as a pilot, there was no way he would be available for his manager. Other days, when he was not flying, he would be very involved with his franchise. These were subtle factors in his ideal semi-absentee ownership model that helped lead him to a franchise that had systems in place to make this possible.

## Why Would Someone Want to Be a Semi-Absentee Owner?

Now that you understand more about semi-absentee ownership, you might be wondering ... what is the attraction?

Most of the reasons touch on the financial side of this process. Someone with a well-paying job who is the breadwinner of their household might find it too difficult to step away from their corporate job and paycheck and jump straight into business ownership. But they still have the goal of gaining more control over their life and see owning the franchise as a secondary revenue stream that will lead to their eventual exit strategy from the corporate world.

So as the franchise grows to the point where you *do* feel safe leaving that corporate job ... then what?

(Remember, you do not *have* to leave your job ever. But many people see franchise ownership as a long-term exit strategy from the corporate world.)

Do you meet with your manager, the one who worked like crazy to build YOUR franchise to the point where you can quit your job, and say, "Thanks for everything, but I've got it from here ... you're fired!"?

I mean, you could. But typically, that is not the right thing to do. There are two general paths ...

1. The owner keeps everything in place and running smoothly with the existing franchise and then finds a second franchise to launch. Perhaps the owner runs that second franchise full time, or perhaps they hire another manager and essentially become the semi-absentee owner of two franchises.

2. The more common path is that the owner focuses on growing the existing franchise and adding more locations

or territories. At that point, the owner may choose to be much more hands-on and dive into the minutiae, but usually, they will stay at a high level, managing all of the pieces on the board.

### *Diversification*

Another factor in the attractiveness of semi-absentee ownership is diversification. Some people use the semi-absentee franchise ownership option as a way to diversify their investments and revenue streams. Whether they have a good job that they do not intend to leave or they are an entrepreneur juggling multiple ventures, for these people, a semi-absentee franchise is a way to control the return they get on investments.

People with this mindset see a 401(k) or stock market investment as a conservative option but one in which they have no CONTROL over. A franchise, however, is completely within their control. There is the potential to reap higher rewards than if the return is left up to the volatile market.

### *Becoming a Semi-Absentee Owner*

Whatever your personal reasons for considering semi-absentee franchise ownership, the fact remains that this is an attractive option for many people. But as we have established, semi-absentee models differ greatly from one franchise to the next. It is important to find the model that best aligns with your ideal role, available time, and accessibility as an owner.

How do you find that ideal franchise? That is where a franchise coach, or franchise advisor, can help. Our team at FranCoach is one great example, but there are many others out there as well.

Whoever you choose to work with, it is important to look for a coach with experience in this industry who will truly be able to give you a behind-the-scenes look into the varied semi-absentee structures of the different brands you might be considering. Working with a trustworthy and knowledgeable franchise coach is typically the first step toward success as a franchise owner, because you will be set up to succeed in a franchise that is really right for YOU.

## CHAPTER 9

# Fear of Failure

## What If I Fail?

Whether people vocalize it or not, failure is something that crosses almost everyone's mind while considering franchise ownership. Do not run from this fear. Instead, let's lean into a bit to determine whether you will, in fact, fail.

Let's review the most important factors in one's success (or failure) as a franchise owner ...

First off, you need to **follow the plan**! This should be obvious and easy to do, but that does not mean people cannot find a way to screw up a great plan. Even when deviating from the plan or ignoring it altogether means you are putting your own money in jeopardy, there will always be people out there who will do so. Don't be that person. If you cannot or will not follow a plan, then please do not become a franchise owner. Stick with your job or start something on your own from scratch.

Second, you must **put forth the required effort**. If you are going to be a full-time owner ... act like it. Work 40 hours a week. No franchise expects you to work 80 to 100 hours per week. And if I ever hear an owner say they are, I will tell them that they are either lying, bad at math, or are not following the plan (most likely the part about hiring a team).

If you are a semi-absentee owner, your required effort will be fewer hours—but you still need to commit to them. If you need to be spending 15 hours per week on the franchise as a semi-absentee owner and you only spend three hours per week, there is a good chance the business will struggle.

If your failure as a franchise owner is because of not following the plan or not putting forth the required effort, there is only one person to blame for this. Here is a hint … it is not the franchisor!

The other way one might fail as a franchise owner is not finding the best fit. The first two reasons, which we have just covered, should be really easy to avoid. But as you have learned in this book, there are tons of factors that go into finding your best fit—and mistakes here can be costly.

If you find yourself owning a franchise that does not pass your Get Out of Bed Test, then it can be challenging to reach the goals you had for franchise ownership … not the least of which is just your overall happiness.

### How Can I Conquer My Fear of Failure?

When our team has a client who is vetting franchisors but also struggling with the fear of failure, we typically coach them on a few things.

First, we will review with the client what they like about a given franchise. Usually, this happens when the other options we introduced to them have been eliminated. Once we narrow it down to one franchise left standing, things start to get real. It is not uncommon for people to hyperventilate a little bit and say, "Wait, am I REALLY about to do this?"

As we go through this recap, we tend to hear a lot of excitement and energy. Everything sounds so good to the client, and they are able to see themselves getting out of bed to run this business every day. But this excitement tends to lead them to wonder, "What's the catch?"

Maybe that franchise is just really good at "selling" their brand to people. Maybe the four owners that you talked to during Validation Calls were the only four owners in the system who are not failing miserably. Maybe the franchisor has just completely lied to you about everything.

Are these concerns possible? Sure they are. Are they remotely likely? Not really. But when fear creeps into our minds, no matter how much we want to ignore the problem and hope it goes away, we need to address it. So how do we address the fear of failure?

I typically prompt clients to literally ask the franchisor (and potentially one of their owners), "Why would someone fail while owning this franchise?"

What answer are you going to hear from the franchisor? Well, they could say, "No clue! We don't really care if you make it or not!"—but they won't.

What will happen is that you are going to get a long answer, and the first two things that every single franchisor will say are ...

You might fail if you:

1. Don't follow the plan
2. Don't put forth the required effort

Now, that might be somewhat helpful, but it will probably not be enough to squash your fear. This is when the franchisor's answer will get really long, because they are going to tell you the specifics of *their* franchise.

Let's say you are looking at owning an in-home senior care franchise. You are talking to the franchisor about why someone might fail as an owner with their brand. The franchisor will follow up a comment about following the plan and putting forth the effort by saying that an owner might fail if they:

- Cannot or do not want to build a big team
- Does not care about customer service and building long-term relationships with clients and referral sources
- Do not give a damn about making an impact in the community and are just trying to make money regardless of what people think
- Hate old people.

Keep in mind that these are just for our senior care example. As the franchisor talks about the specific things that might make someone fail as an owner of their brand, you are going to think one of two things.

If you think, "Wow, they just described me to a T," you should run as fast and as far away from that franchise as possible because it is clearly not the right fit for YOU!

Alternately, you will hear all of that and think some version of, "Duh, of course an owner of a senior care franchise would fail if that described them." You, on the other hand, have the opposite of those characteristics! Hearing why someone else might fail can be great confirmation that YOU won't, because you do not share those traits. Had you ignored the fear of failure and hoped it would just go away (Hint: It wouldn't.), then you would not have been able to reach the level of confidence and calmness that shows that you have found your match.

The other factor to consider is your own history. If you look at the franchise and see how you fit what they want in an owner, you like the people and the culture of the brand, and you know you will follow the plan and put forth the effort, then what is left?

In short, your track record.

Ask yourself this: How many times in your professional life have you been a massive failure? (Again, *professional* life!) Most people who are even considering franchise ownership are smart, successful people, so the answer to how many times they have been a massive failure is usually zero.

Why is that? Because they have been in roles that fit what they were good at and what they wanted to do. These non-failure professional experiences often lead to some level of advancement in their job—either a pay increase, a promotion, or both. Even when someone looks back and sees a professional failure, they quickly see how that role was a bad fit for them.

I remember a job that I failed miserably at right out of college. I sold Cutco knives … but not for long, because I was terrible at it. I sold one knife. Not one knife set. One KNIFE. And that was only because the dad of one of my good friends took pity on me and bought one. It is not that selling knives is a bad job (actually, this might be debatable!) and it is not that I am a miserable failure … it means that selling knives was a terrible match for me. My Get Out of Bed Test was a total miss—think waking up at 10 a.m. and rolling back over for a couple more hours.

So when you wonder if you might fail … lean into it. Ask yourself, what is it that you really like about the franchise that you are almost ready to commit to? Does it get you excited? Do you wish you were waking up tomorrow and owning it? Are you going to follow the plan and put forth the effort? Did asking the franchisor why you might fail only validate that you won't?

If so, the only question left is … are you ready to bet on yourself and take control of your life? And, if that is the case, what are you waiting for?

## What Are the Traits of Strong Franchise Owners?

If you are worrying about failure, it may help you to remember some key traits that successful franchise owners share. If you see yourself reflected in these characteristics, the chances are that franchise ownership could be a good fit for you. Here are some of the qualities that are common between successful owners …

### #1: FSO

"FSO" is one of the most important acronyms we discuss with our clients and it stands for … Figure Stuff Out. Honestly, we use a different S-word—but you get the point!

Wait a second. First, you tell me that all I need to do is follow the plan and put forth the required effort to be a franchise owner, and now you are telling me that I need to FSO, too? How is that possible?

Yes, it is true that the franchisor will have a very detailed plan for your success and will have tons of training and ongoing support … but that only gets you so far.

What if you roll into your sandwich franchise one Saturday and realize that somehow the order for napkins got messed up or that three people have called in sick on the same day? Then what? Who are you going to call on Saturday at the franchise headquarters? Where in the training manual is the process for "no napkins on Saturday"?

It is not in the training manual. This is where your leadership skills and your desire to be at the top of the food chain come into play.

To be a successful franchise owner, you need to want to have the ball in your hands. You need to *want* to figure stuff out, be in control, and build your business into a successful one.

### #2: Follow the Plan and Put Forth the Effort

Remember, NOT doing these two things is the main reason you could fail as a franchise owner. Every single franchisor will tell you the same thing. As a franchisor, you MUST:

1. Follow the plan.
2. Put forth the required effort.

If you can do those two things, you are halfway to success already.

### #3: Leadership

To put it simply, why would you own a franchise if you do not enjoy being a leader? This goes back to your history of success and your ability to FSO on the fly. Forgive the sports analogy, but do you want the ball in your hands at the end of the game to take the last shot? Are you comfortable making decisions and being in the driver's seat?

Successful (and happy) franchise owners are good leaders. And an important part of effective leadership is ...

### #4: Positivity

Why does positivity matter? The fact is, owning a franchise is not all rainbows and unicorns. Things *will* go wrong. That is where the ability to FSO comes in, and positivity goes right along with it.

When things do go wrong, if your reaction is always one of negativity, it is easy for the problem to be magnified or to spiral out of control. People with a negative attitude also tend to foreshadow problems. Then, when one arises, their responses begin with something like, "Ugh, I *knew* this was going to happen." Or you might hear a negative person pointing out a number of problems without offering up any sort of solution.

This attitude can wear on a franchise owner to the point of not even being able to see or celebrate their successes—and oftentimes, it can create a toxic work environment. After all, who wants to be around Eeyore all day?

When an owner can combine a positive attitude with the ability to FSO, they will bolster confidence among their team and their customers, too. A negative person will see a problem as a mountain that probably can't be climbed. A positive person will see the same problem as a mere speed bump and maybe even a fun challenge to overcome.

For instance, let's go back to the napkin example that we mentioned earlier. If the negative owner shows up to their sandwich franchise and realizes they are out of napkins, it might ruin the whole day for the owner and surely for their staff. The napkin issue will be talked about all day and the owner will be sure that their business will suffer due to not having the proper napkins or having none at all.

The positive owner, on the other hand, will already have a contingency plan. Perhaps there is an owner of the same franchise across town that they can buy some napkins from. Or maybe they run to the nearest grocery store to buy some temporary napkins to hold the sandwich shop over in the meantime. Then, the owner will make sure that more napkins are en route in the next supply shipment. Either way, napkins will quickly be procured and the napkin issue will not be the toxic topic of the day.

There is a quote from the fourteenth Dalai Lama that illustrates this mindset perfectly:

"If a problem is fixable, if a situation is such that you can do something about it, then there is no need to worry. If it's not fixable, then there is no help in worrying. There is no benefit in worrying whatsoever."

If you have these traits (the ability to FSO, a commitment to following the plan and putting in the work, leadership abilities, and a positive attitude) then you have what it takes to be a successful franchise owner.

## CHAPTER 10

# The Final Steps

### How Will I Know?

To quote the late, great Whitney Houston ... "How will I know?" You have determined that franchise ownership is an attractive, attainable path for you. You have thoroughly vetted a few different franchises, and now you have narrowed them down to one or two final contenders. So how will you know, *for certain*, that you are ready to move forward?

At this point, what you are waiting for is the last step in the Discovery Process. As we mentioned earlier, this is commonly referred to as either "Discovery Day" or "Meet the Team Day." So what is this?

Well, this is a day in which you will meet the team of that particular franchisor. Clever title, right? Most of the time, this is in person, but some franchisors will do these virtually.

### More About Meet the Team Day

Virtual Meet the Team Days are usually video meetings that are several hours long. The in-person versions tend to cover two days. The first day typically entails just the evening and a dinner with members of their leadership team and any other candidates who are attending besides you. This is a casual way to get to know their team as well as the other potential owners there with you.

As always with this process, the franchise is vetting you too—so we like to advise people not to revert back to their college days. This is not the time to pull out a beer bong or try to break the record for most tequila shots without needing your stomach pumped. Sure, that was fun in college … but we are too old for that now. Plus, our professors were not there watching us and considering that display in our final grade.

The second day of an in-person Meet the Team Day typically takes place at the franchisor's headquarters. This is a chance to see everything and meet everyone. There will be presentations from each department.

For instance, the franchise development person you have been working with surely talked to you about the marketing, and that was great, but now you get to hear directly from the head of marketing and meet their team. You will learn more about the marketing plan, how that team will support you, and maybe even some key metrics. You will get a chance to ask questions and hear what other candidates ask as well.

At the end of the day, if your head has not exploded from a wealth of helpful information, the franchise will let you know their timeline to award you the franchise (or not). Sometimes, they will tell you at the end of the day. Other times, they may meet as a team and set up a call with you once you are back home.

(If they do tell you while you are there, do not worry—this is not a timeshare situation where you cannot escape the room until you write a check.)

Either way, the important part is that YOU will know. It will truly be so crystal clear at that point that you will either run to the airport screaming, "Get me away from these crazy people!" or you will be headed there with a big smile on your face KNOWING that you have found the right franchise for you to own.

Really, at the end of this journey, the right franchise for you will be so obvious that you will not even have to make a decision. I know this sounds crazy, but it happens every single time. With all of the vetting, preparation, and education you have done throughout this process, you will *know* at the end of the day whether or not franchise ownership is right for you.

### Should My Spouse Be Involved?

Let's talk about the elephant in the room … and no, we are not calling your spouse fat.

There are times we work with clients who are married and are looking for a business for themselves. They go through the process of working with us at FranCoach and vetting franchisors during the Discovery Process, and never involve their spouses. Is it possible that this works out just fine, their spouse never ever wants to be included in this journey, AND they are 100 percent fine with their other half investing hundreds of thousands of dollars into a franchise?

Yes, it is possible. But is it likely? Not so much.

What is more likely is that, when the spouse gets wind of the fact that their partner is *really* serious about this, they scuttle the whole thing. Usually that sounds something like this …

- "Wait, you are about to do WHAT with our money?"
- "Franchises all fail."
- "Franchises don't make any money."
- "What do YOU know about THAT industry?"

I worked with a client whose spouse literally said, "Over my dead body." Another one threatened divorce.

Here is the thing about a franchise: Even if your spouse never works a day in it, it is still the family business.

The other thing to remember is that the Discovery Process is nothing like the corporate interview process.

Imagine this: You show up to a big job interview and you ask your future boss, "Hey, is it okay if my wife sits in on the interview?" Let me give you a hint: That interview is not going to go well. I mean, bringing your wife to an interview might be slightly better than bringing your mom to an interview—but that is not a job you are going to get!

With the Discovery Process, it is the complete opposite. The spouse, even if they never work a day in the business, will be welcome to participate in every step of the journey. At FranCoach, we always encourage this. Why? There are a couple of reasons.

First, imagine that you are on a call with a franchisor and they are telling you all about their marketing plan. This is ALL brand-new information to you. As you hear it, it all makes sense and it makes you feel confident that you will not have any problems finding customers if you become an owner.

But then, you go to tell your partner all about it. You are seriously pumped … but as you start to explain the marketing plan, you realize you do not remember everything exactly as the franchisor said it. After all, you have heard this information only one time, whereas the person working with the franchise has said it all hundreds of times. There is no way you can relay it as accurately as they can.

The more gaps you introduce as you share a pared-down version of the information, the more questions your spouse is going to have. And they are not going to be asking the "seeking information" type of questions. Instead, they are going to be asking the "poking holes" type of questions, and those are rarely fun. The more holes there are, the more doubt and skepticism your spouse will have.

But, if they *are* on the calls with you, then they will get the full picture and hear all of the same information that you are receiving. It is that you are trying to deceive your spouse while relaying information (please do not try this at home, boys and girls), but there is just no way that you can share all of the information accurately.

Second, if you have your spouse on calls with the franchisors, they will also be able to come up with questions that you probably never would have thought of. In my case, that is because my wife is way smarter than I am—but also, she is going to hear things differently and have different concerns and fears to address. It will benefit everyone to have both spouses feeling confident in the franchisor of choice.

When your spouse is involved throughout (or at least some of the time) it will help their level of excitement and, oftentimes, they will start to see how the franchise is a really great fit for you and your skill set.

Plus, your spouse can be your biggest cheerleader. Let's say you and your spouse are on calls together, learning about the franchise ownership process and the specifics of a given brand. At some point, your spouse is going to start bragging about you. They are going to share why you will be so amazing as a franchise owner, how this role fits you perfectly, and so on. Let's be honest: That is great information for the franchisor to hear. Plus, it can further squash your fear of failure!

Now, not every spouse will have the time and the flexibility to be on calls with the franchisors. That is totally understandable. So how can you involve them if that is the case?

If you have a webinar with a franchisor and they have a PowerPoint presentation, for instance, ask if they are willing to share that resource with you so that you can share it with your spouse. In most cases, they will not only be fine with this but also happy to do so!

There is also the option to have a "catch-up call" later in the Discovery Process. As we start to narrow things down to one franchise, the spouse can jump on one call, during which the franchisor might go back and cover information in a brief overview—really, this will be an opportunity for the franchisor to answer any questions the spouse has and to get them up to speed. The "catch-up call" can be very helpful for a busy spouse, because it does not inconvenience them while still involving them in the journey.

The one part of the Discovery Process that we *highly* recommend the spouse participate in is the Meet the Team Day. This can cause a bit of a sacrifice in terms of childcare for couples with kids, but it is incredibly valuable for both spouses to attend. One of the biggest things you learn from Meet the Team Day is the insight into the people within a franchise. You will want your spouse to use their "spidey senses" to evaluate the people you will be working with.

In most cases, a franchise will require the spouse to make at least one appearance. If both of you attending Meet the Team Day is not possible, maybe that looks like showing up for a "catch-up call." Again, remember that the franchisor is vetting you too. Knowing that you have support from your other half can be a crucial component of success.

## What If My Spouse Will Be an Owner, Too?

If both spouses are going to be equally involved, it is basically required that both people participate in every step of the Discovery Process.

One big thing that we prompt couples to think about is defining their respective roles in a franchise. Knowing who is doing what is always important as a franchise owner, but even more so when you are partnered with your spouse.

As an owner and a boss, your staff expect you to tell them what to do and give them feedback on their performance. Telling your *spouse* what to do in your shared business and then trying to give them feedback on their performance seems a bit dicey.

I am no marriage counselor, but I feel like bossing my wife around and then telling her where she messed up is a recipe for needing a therapist … or a divorce attorney. So, how do we handle this?

First off, even before you become franchise owners, role definition needs to be discussed and ironed out. In most cases, business partners (whether they are married to each other or not) tend to have more complementary skills than overlapping skills. But it is not uncommon for partners to have some things that they are either both good at or both do not want to do.

Think about this concept around your house. If you and your spouse both love doing dishes and hate taking out the trash, you are going to have the cleanest dishes in town but trash everywhere. Someone needs to suck it up and take out the trash. The same thing goes for your business. Not everything an owner does is glamorous. Sometimes, you might have to take out the trash.

As spouses in business together, before signing a Franchise Agreement, you must determine who is doing what, who is in charge of what, and who has decision-making power over what. That way, there will be no gray area once you get started. The role definition is key to both a happy business partnership and, more importantly, continuing to be happily married.

The same can be said for when a parent and their adult child are business partners. We have had a few clients go into business with their parents or children as franchise owners. Again, role definition is key, because you are partners … you are not their parent when it comes to the business and you want to be careful not to blur these lines.

As a parent, "Because I said so" is a reason that we get away with saying. As a business partner, this reason is not one that should be used. Take the time to define roles and have the respect to stay in your lanes. When you do that, both the business relationship and the personal one will thrive.

## What Else Do I Need to Seal the Deal?

Let's back up for a minute … before you attend Meet the Team Day, there is some preparation that needs to be done. We typically advise our clients to complete four key things before attending a Meet the Team Day.

Why? These four elements will make things as smooth and efficient as possible *after* Meet the Team Day. Think about it like this: When you are excited and certain that you have found the best franchise for you to own and cannot wait to get started, will you really want a bunch of hurdles standing in your way afterward that will slow you down?

The good news is that these four things can easily be taken care of beforehand!

### #1: Validation Calls

These calls should be completed before you attend Meet the Team Day. As we discussed earlier in this book, Validation Calls are when you get to talk to existing owners of a given franchise. Usually, we recommend that, to get a complete picture, you talk to three or four owners with diverse backgrounds and tenures as owners.

### #2: Territories and Mapping

A "territory" refers to the area that you serve as a franchisee. Where is your territory and how many will you have? Even a brick-and-mortar franchise will have a territory or bubble that will be yours. Have you reviewed this with the franchisor? Are you comfortable with which and how many territories you will start with?

Occasionally, there might be a minor tweak to this after Meet the Team Day. For the most part, however, you will want to solidify your territories beforehand, because this information will be included in your Franchise Agreement.

### #3: Funding

How are you funding this franchise, if you are awarded it? Is it an SBA (Small Business Administration) Loan? Are you using the ROBS (Rollovers as Business Start-ups) program? Whatever the funding option, you need to know which one and to have confirmed that you are eligible. For instance, if you are going to get an SBA loan, you will want pre-approval for the amount needed to launch your franchise. Most franchisors will require this confirmation before you attend. You do not need to actually *have* the SBA loan or have completed the rollover for the ROBS program before Meet the Team Day, but you must know how you plan to fund the franchise.

### *#4: Document Review*

You will need to review the FDD and the Franchise Agreement. Reviewing the FDD typically happens in the first half of the Discovery Process, so that should have been done already. The Franchise Agreement is typically not reviewed until closer to the end ... but, if you are about to attend Meet the Team Day, then guess what? You are close to the end!

Let's dive a little deeper into what you can expect when reviewing these two documents.

## Where Do I Sign?

As we get to the end of the franchise Discovery Process (and the end of this book), it is important to cover the two crucial documents you will want to review before attending Meet the Team Day: the FDD and the Franchise Agreement.

Franchisors very rarely negotiate any terms in the Franchise Agreement. On the slim chance that they do, I can assure you that they are NOT negotiating the Franchise Fee or royalties. I am sure you are a crack negotiator ... but, in this instance, it ain't happening.

So then why review it? Well, it is important to review the Franchise Agreement because it outlines your responsibilities to the franchisor and theirs to you. Most people read through the Franchise Agreement and can come up with a few questions to go over with the franchisor. Typically, this conversation can provide enough clarity that you are comfortable signing if you are awarded the franchise.

However, if you are more comfortable with having an expert review the Franchise Agreement for you, now is the time to acquire a franchise attorney. I cannot emphasize the word "franchise" enough here. This is not the time to call your Uncle Bob who used to practice family law.

The legal profession (like the medical profession) is highly specialized. If you are going through a divorce, you do not call the accident attorney who got you a great settlement when you were in that fender bender. But, if you do, good luck having anything other than the shirt on your back when the divorce is finalized.

A franchise attorney can provide an expert legal opinion on the Franchise Agreement. Are you about to get totally screwed by this franchise? Or is everything in here standard language seen in 4,000 other Franchise Agreements? Mostly, the franchise attorney will provide clarity on the language and give you the peace of mind that you are properly protected as a franchise owner. As a result, you will better understand what is expected of you as a franchise owner and what is expected from the franchisor. If you are going to have a legal review, you want to do this before Meet the Team Day to give you time to review any outstanding questions with the franchisor.

Ultimately, the only thing you want on your mind at Meet the Team Day is confirming that this is the right franchise for you. If so, you want everything in place to sign, fund, and start your business as soon as possible.

---

CHAPTER 11

---

# Starting Your Franchise Journey

## What Now?

In the course of this book, we have covered the ins and outs of becoming a franchise owner. We have discussed why this is an attractive opportunity, what experience you need (and do not need), how to find the best franchise for YOU, how much it costs, how much money you can make ... and so much more.

If you have made it this far, the chances are that your interest is piqued. So let's take a little quiz to help you determine if you are in the right place ...

**1. Do you want more control over your life?**
Are you dreaming of control over your freedom and flexibility, the things you do every day, and the people you are around? Do you want control over the money you make now and in the future? Would you like the ability to build wealth and equity? Would you like to provide a legacy for your family?

## 2. Are you willing and able to follow a proven plan?

Are you able to commit to following the franchisor's plan but still be resourceful and figure things out when you need to? Will you tap into resources when you need help?

## 3. Are you dedicated and driven enough to put forth the required effort?

Are you a good leader? Are you positive enough not to get derailed when things go wrong? (And yes, things do go wrong from time to time. Owning a franchise is not all rainbows and unicorns!)

## 4. Do you have a track record of professional success that you can fall back on?

Have you experienced success in your career in jobs or roles that allowed your skill set to shine? However, that success does not need to be job-related. Maybe you have excellent school transcripts or have experienced athletic triumphs.

## 5. Do you have support from family and friends?

Having a strong support network of family and friends (and yes, also your spouse) is a big component of success as a franchise owner. And finally …

## 6. What are you going to do now?

We have discussed some key questions and identified areas for you to think about as you consider franchise ownership, and we have even shared some of our team's secrets. You know what questions to ask along the way, and you know to keep an open mind as you explore franchise options you might not have considered otherwise.

We have also shared how a franchise coach can help you throughout this entire journey at no cost to you.

If you answered "yes" to the questions above, then franchise ownership really might be the path for you. Whether you go it alone or find a great franchise coach to help you (Hint: FranCoach!), the next step is yours. Once you get started down this path, you might find that at the end of the journey, your better tomorrow is waiting.

# Index

www.ingramcontent.com/pod-product-compliance
Lightning Source LLC
Jackson TN
JSHW011853230225
79432JS00003B/3